# *Dedication*

This book is dedicated to my sons, Ed and Josh. They have taught me more about life, leadership, teamwork, and integrity than I can ever truly explain. My gratitude is profound, only surpassed by my love for them.

Professor James Porterfield from Stanford Graduate School of Business taught me that "all businesses are the same, they are intended to gain and retain customers profitably to create shareholder value." I will always be grateful for having had his guidance.

This book is also dedicated to all the amazing mentors, team members and customers that I have had along the way. Each one has taught me so much. It's an honor to share what I learned from them with my students, clients and friends. This body of knowledge I have gained is at the heart of this book.

Last, but not least, none of this would have happened in a timely fashion without my associate, David Deutschman.

*The One Day MBA© Published July 2018*

# Table of Contents

*This book is part of the "One Day MBA" program designed by Lew Jaffe. It has a supporting video series that includes a deeper dive into in the content contained in this book, plus master classes on Negotiating & Real Estate.*

**Go to "TheOneDayMBA.org" to learn more about the video program.**

## *Forward*

This book is designed to help you focus on what is truly important as you grow your career or business. It is made up of lessons that I've learned through both my successes and my failures. You may find that some of the things I share sound like clichés or platitudes; however, they are designed to help you better understand and remember what I share. All the stories are either firsthand or have been shared with me by some of the amazing people I have come across in my life. Some of the contents contained here is similar to what you will hear form other successful business leaders and coaches, that's because these things work, if you just take action and implement them into your life and behaviors at work.

To get the most out of this book, read it with an open mind and know that, while some of the lessons shared here you may have heard before, for some reason they didn't connect with you. Hopefully, I have presented them in such a way that you can incorporate them into how you think and act as both a person and a businessperson. I truly believe that you cannot be a good businessperson if you're not also genuinely a good person. Much of the content in the book is designed for both.

I know we've all come across bad people who seem to be successful; however, they are the exception to the rule. It's not you, I know this because you are reading this book, perfecting your skills.

The goal in this book is that, by the end, you will:

1.  Know you have what it takes to be successful.

2.  Gain a better understanding of how everything connects, and nothing is ever in a vacuum. I use the word ecosystem to describe this effect.

3.  Better understand how people perceive you and then use that knowledge to perfect the way you communicate to get things accomplished.

4.  Learn the difference between what is important and what is interesting, so that you can focus on the right things at the right time.

5.  Have new tools in your toolbox, so you can better address issues and resolve them more quickly.

6.  Believe that number one (1) in this list is true!

This book is written and should be read as a dialogue between the two of us. It's personal; I want you to be a success! I decided to become a business professor four years ago because I wanted to make a difference in students' lives. I am invested in your success and my only goal here is to take you to the next level in your career, regardless of where you are on your career path.

I will be repetitive as to certain concepts and constructs, as I want to emphasize points and illustrate how the concepts are all related. The more you understand that there is an ecosystem to business, and that you have the power to impact that ecosystem, the more successful you will become in your career.

# Chapter 1: The Success Mindset

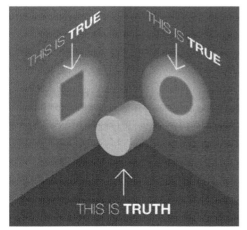

The word "Mindset" is overused. However, in the context of business, it is particularly salient. Whether you are a Manager, Owner or CEO, your path must start with a winning mindset. You may be wondering, "What does that mean?"

I will share a story from early in my career. My company had burned through most of its cash, the technology finally worked, and we had a new venture capitalist ready to invest. During the demonstration, the technology worked flawlessly, both the hardware and the code base. The hardware was running hotter than planned and, as a result, we accidently started a small fire in the VC's office. The potential investor walked out of the room, frankly, in an agitated state.

On the ride back to the airport to head home, I admit I was in tears, worried about running out of money. My partner, on the other hand, was joyous. He kept saying to me, "Did you see that, it worked perfectly." I kept saying, "Didn't you see the fire?" We went back and forth. Finally, I got it, he knew we could resolve the heat problem. I was focused on the failure. He was focused on the future and I was stuck in the past. I was wrong!

The next morning, my partner forced me to call the VC and ask for the money. Once again, I asked him if he saw the fire; he said, "It's not a problem." I called the VC hoping it would go straight to voicemail. Shockingly, he answered.

I hesitantly asked him if he could fund us, and that if he chose to do so, he could deduct the cost of the new rug from the price. To make a long story short, he said yes. He was impressed that I had the courage to call him, he said it took grit and he respected grit.

There was so much power in my partner's approach. At first, I was too emotional to get it. We were in the same room, we saw the technology work, and we saw the fire. However, it became clear that focusing on the part that would enable our end game of getting funding was the correct approach to achieve our goal.

That was my first lesson about the "entrepreneurial mindset."

At first, this was difficult for me to comprehend. There are always multiple ways of looking at a situation. Additionally, there are a set of emotions that we attach to the event. The event itself is neutral, I know that sounds crazy. The point here is, we get to consciously choose which emotions we attach and the perspective we take. This impacts our actions, as well as how long it takes to implement the actions. If this is true, which it is, then we have a choice.

Wallow in failure or focus on the fix. One may feel better in that moment. But, the momentary reaction adds no value, while the other gets you back on track. For some people, like my partner, this was his nature. For me, it was learned behavior. It took practice to get there, and that may be the case for you. Regardless of your path, it is a critical success factor to have the strength to take a step back, focus on actions that get you where you need to be, and **implement them.**

We have all heard the infamous glass saying: Is the glass half full or half empty? Same glass, but with two different perspectives. Becoming open minded and exploring multiple perspectives around one event can be eye opening.

Stay positive and search for solutions. Not blindly positive, but a focused positive towards driving the successful outcome. Just think, the answer is always NO if you never ask. So why not ask?

From that day on, I always focused on what was important, instead of what got in the way of success. I have been blessed with an amazing career that has allowed me the opportunity to retire, teach at a prestigious business school, and share lessons I've learned, with you.

Keep an open mind as you read this book. Some of the ideas and tools presented will immediately make sense; others may need a little time to set in. I promise, these practical lessons will get you far in your career. Jack Welch, the former CEO of General Electric once said, "Don't lose yourself on the way to the top." This book is designed to both help you find your "top," give you the tools to get there, and help you stay on track so you don't get lost.

All the lessons come from my successes and failures. There is so much to be gained from examining failure. Never ignore failure; explore what went wrong. I've also included lessons I've learned from my mentors. Every career and every success comes from a team, in one way or another. This is why I've included what I learned from my team along the way. I honor them by sharing all of our lessons with you, the reader. Everyone goes through their own entrepreneurial journey. Stay open to the possibilities, use these lessons, remember these stories, and your skills will surely grow.

Let's GO!

*What makes building a business so complicated?*

People and physics. Entropy is a concept in physics that states: "Everything runs to a state of disorder unless you put energy into the system." People build businesses; therefore, if you put the right energy and direction towards the people involved in a business, order will follow as a result.

To destroy the negative impact of entropy, focus that energy, your energy, on the following sentence: **"All businesses are the same, gain and retain customers, profitably, in order to create shareholder value."** The simplicity and importance that comes from the underlying concept in this sentence is profound. Everything is about focusing on customers, profits and value. It lets you know where to focus your efforts, vision and team. These are the principles that drive enterprises to greatness.

Think about it. If a company has no customers, it has no business. If you can't make the business profitable, it will not be sustainable. Your job as an entrepreneur or intrapreneur is to keep your team focused on this simple sentence "*gain and retain customers, profitably, in order to create shareholder value*" and all of its meaning. Focus on getting and keeping customers profitably and your business will thrive.

Let's take a moment and define intrapreneur. If one "owns their job," and treats the company as though it's theirs regardless of their equity stake, they are an intrapreneur. It is a mindset that will get you noticed, promoted and drive you towards a successful career.

Business does not need to be complicated, nor should you make it complicated for your team or your customers.

Never forget how you want to be treated when you are the customer. Treat your customers with the respect and care that you demand when are the buyer.

*Can you separate being a good businessperson from being a good person?*

This is a question that is asked of me over and over. The answer is complicated, yet simple. It's your choice. Each choice has implications, so I will make it easy: for those who want to learn from my experience and perspective, which has a proven track record, the answer is "you must be a good person to be a good businessperson."

To be truly successful, you must walk the walk, not just talk the talk. Today's employees and team members are becoming more and more sophisticated. If you want to make great things happen, your team must be inspired. If you want people to do what you need from them, you must clearly communicate a purpose and vision. If you are not in alignment with that vision, everyone will see it and run the other way. This alignment is the baseline for being a good businessperson and that's the same thing as being a good person.

If you treat your team in a manner that you would never allow yourself to be treated, how can you expect them to be loyal and dedicated long term? They have the right and if you lead correctly, the obligation to hold you accountable for their success and you hold them accountable for yours. Accountability is not blame! Accountability is ownership. As a team, you rise and fall together. Share the wins, take responsibility for the team and its failure. This mindset and behavior drives small and grand successes. This builds relationships, which are at the center of making progress toward goals.

For a while, they might stay for a pay check. They might look for work while you are paying them. But, they are not going to be working for your customers, your mission, and clearly not for the value that you are trying to create.

As the leader, you have only one "tool" that drives success, and that is communication. It's not just your words; it's your actions, not only when you are being observed, but also, when no one is looking.

*What are the most important things to focus on that drive success?*

Business is an "ecosystem" in which everything is interconnected. The elements that I focus on are what I call the 7Cs: Cash, Customers, Culture, Change, Clock, Cooperation, and Communication. The awareness of this interconnectivity is step one. When properly managed together, they will help you drive your company and your team to where you need them to go.

Cash

Cash is the life blood of a company. It supports the company's health and growth, just like blood does in the human body. Think of cash like the fuel for a car. You can only drive forward if you have the necessary amount of fuel. When you run out of fuel, the journey is over. Because cash is a limited resource it must be tracked, managed and properly deployed. You can only spend a dollar in one place. Where you will get the best return from that dollar has to be front of mind. Your focus must always be how much money will spending that dollar yield.

Customers

Customers are cash waiting to happen. When a customer buys your goods and pays your bill, you get more cash (fuel) to drive forward. However, you only get more cash if your business model is profitable, and the customer is satisfied. The cost of acquiring a customer is high; however, the cost of losing a customer is even higher. Satisfied customers tell some people how happy they are; dissatisfied customers tell EVERYONE how unhappy they are. Successful companies know: who their customers are, where to find them, how to satisfy them and most importantly, how to make a profit from them.

## Culture

Corporate culture is the driver behind how we all interact in a company. Look at the first four letters in the word culture, they spell "CULT." What is the cult in your organization? How do you treat your customers? How do you treat your fellow team members? How do you treat your vendors? This internal cult makes a difference in how people see your brand, their desire to work with you, your ability to attract and retain great talent, and yes, even generate cash. Remember, a culture that drives constant improvement is one that drives profits.

## Change

The only constant in life and business is change. You should expect that the business environment will always be changing. Customers demand and expect change, competition finds new ways to become more competitive, and employers find new ways to attract and retain high performers. Successful companies need to embrace change. While change is hard and scary, resisting change can be expensive and, over time, futile. Remember, time and money are finite resources, resisting change will burn through those resources and making your organization weaker. Anticipating change on the other hand will position you and or your company to be well positioned to capitalize on these changes. Another powerful tool is creating a corporate culture that embraces change. Staying nimble, and adaptive saves resources and drives progress in a cost-effective manor over time.

## Clock

In addition to cash, the most perishable asset a company has is time. The most perishable we all have as human beings is time. If you can do it today, do it today. Often, we act like time is not valuable, especially if we have procrastinating tendencies. Wasting time is the exact opposite of the mindset that enables success.

If you respect time and its value, it's a set in the right direction. This mindset makes more room tomorrow for innovation, productivity and new successful endeavors, by accomplishing the things you need to do today. Even better, complete the things you must do today and then do more.

A great example of the value of time is the value of a seat in an airplane. An airplane has a finite number of seats, each seat has a value. However, the second the door closes for takeoff, any empty seat has zero value. That's the same principle with time, once it's gone, it is gone. Your role is to create the most value you can from each moment.

Cooperation

Nothing good happens unless everyone is working together as a team. This includes the people in the company, and how people support the company; from lenders to shareholders and vendors to service providers. Think about people in a row boat. If one oar is pulling really hard and the other one is not, the boat will go in circles, making no progress. Working independently with everyone on a different page is inefficient and ineffective. By working together, everyone shares the load and the company progresses in the right direction, much faster.

Communication

Communicate, Communicate, Communicate! Communication is *the* key to success. How else will you get everyone on the same page? Here is where it gets complicated. Many people think communication is "what we say." This is a half-truth. We have two ears and one mouth for a reason. Listening is part of communication and is hard. For example, are you just hearing or just listening in order to reply? Do you process what you heard and add value to it? How about tone and context? When someone is yelling, can you hear the message, or do you focus on the delivery?

What was their body language? Eye contact? These are all essential parts of communication. Poor communication leads to confusion, a lack of cooperation, a loss of customers, and ultimately, a depletion of cash.

The 7Cs connect in very powerful ways. They are all equally important, as one drives the others and they interconnect. Focusing on all the Cs is immensely valuable when striving for success.

*I am management, not sales.*

Get over it - everyone is in sales. Let me prove it to you. As the CEO of public companies, I helped sell products to our customers, I had to sell my vision to my team members. After all, they went home at night and I had to sell a compelling reason for them to come back to work tomorrow. I had to sell investors on buy our stock and not to sell it. I had to sell our lenders why they should extend us credit. I had to sell our vendors on why to give us better terms and pricing.

Whichever job you hold, trust me, you are selling someone ideas, products, or needs.

Let me contradict myself for a moment. Stop selling and, instead, create **buyers**. What I am saying is that your role is to get those you interact with to desire to do business with you, buy into your ideas, and appreciate the value that you add to everything that you do. Nobody wants to be "sold." Good customers want to buy; however, only when the people in sales know how to communicate a clear and concise value proposition.

If you look at the stock market, when people are buying a stock, it drives up the price. When there is "selling pressure," the price goes down. When you buy a car, the salesperson tries to sell you a car, but you always look for a better deal. If that salesperson gets you to believe you need that car, you desire that car, you can't live without that car, then you pay more. It's just human nature.

By no means I am I suggesting that you play people or be disingenuous. It is critical to be your genuine self or others will see right through you, or even worse, never trust you. What I am telling you is that successful executives understand people on the "other side of the desk" and communicate to them in such a way that they perceive value and compassion. It makes for a better relationship and a higher level of cooperation.

*Is the customer always right?*

No. However, they need to be treated as if they are or persuaded to see there is another, better solution to their issue. The customer is the life blood of your company. Without customers, what's your purpose for existing? If that's the case, why would you ever alienate a customer?

Let me share with you what may be a nuance to the concept of a customer. I call it the external customer - someone who buys your goods and/or your services. We understand that type of customer. We need to focus on their needs and make every interaction with them positive and profitable.

There is a second type of customer - the internal customer; in other words, your team members. That is correct, every employee in a company is both a vendor and a customer. Take a moment and think about how this might change a corporate culture.

Here are some examples of what I mean: a salesperson is a customer of the marketing department, as they need to find the best way to identify and communicate to external customers. That same sales person is a vendor to the company; they provide the orders that the company needs to drive business. Another example is at the other end of the business process, the accounts receivable department. They are customers of the billing department, they need completed invoices for them to follow up and collect. They vend cash to the business so that the company can pay its bills.

Building this kind of cooperative organization and seeing the connections between each department capitalizes on the 7Cs. Notice how we just explored the Cs of cash, cooperation, customer, cooperation, communication, clock, and culture.

Everything discussed in this chapter is part of my "entrepreneurial mindset" and core beliefs as to how to do business that drove my career. I know it will drive yours, as well.

## Chapter 2: Everything is Connected

*Just because a successful company did it one way does not make it right; it means those things worked in the past!!*

One of the tests of leadership is the ability to recognize a problem before it becomes an emergency.

I need you to wrap your head around this: success is a "past tense" word. Past success does not guarantee future success! There are great lessons from success. Always explore the failures that drove the successes. There are gems in the failures; they contain valuable and insightful information. Look for patterns, analyze decision making, and understand the reactions from the people with whom you interact. The world around you is evolving. Your customers' desires change, your competitors' offerings change, and your team members change. Future success depends on how you anticipate these changes and how you manage your way through them. Apply the lessons that drove past success to create future success. Just relying on having been successful never drives success and it empowers competitors to use it against you and or your organization.

This is also true for you! If you have been successful, you need to prepare for change in order to stay successful. This does not mean drop the traits that drove your success, just apply them in new ways to stay on top. Always keep your ears and mind open to what is going on around you! If you have not been successful, no worries, here is your chance to change that. Work hard, apply these lessons, and great things will happen in both your career and life.

In this chapter, I will introduce more concepts and start sharing some tools you can implement. Combining the right mindset with the right tool is essential to becoming a great manager, leader, or even owner.

*If you can't measure it, you can't manage it.*

Know your numbers; they serve multiple purposes. Planning is always based on numbers. Tracking your history is done through numbers. The numbers are another way to tell the story. The successes are there, the opportunity for greater successes are there, and the failures are all there. The down side of numbers occurs when either you are tracking the wrong numbers, or when you chose to not believe the numbers.

It is a daunting task to think you must measure everything, so the first tool in your tool box is the knowledge of the drivers of your business and how they all interact. Picking the right drivers is often referred to as the levers that help you manage the business. This will help you to communicate to your team what is truly important to make the company successful.

Communication is a big driver. Associated to, "If you can't measure it, you can't manage it," is the concept of *"inspect what you expect."* These concepts, used in tandem, will get you and your team to align towards your goals.

Yes, these are platitudes, but, that does not make them less true. Let's take a deeper dive into what items need to be managed, how you set the tone in the company around what you are expecting and understanding "why" it is important.

Yet again, the 7Cs play a huge role. Every measure ultimately impacts "Cash," Customers," "Clock," and "Communication."

Before we get to the tools themselves, another key concept is understanding the difference between **important** and **interesting**. In emergency situations, they might refer to this a "triage." Here is an example that makes the point: If you go to the ER with a heart attack and a small cut on the thumb, we all know, the heart attack takes precedence, because it is objectively more threatening and important!

*If you run out of sales, it will result in a slow painful death. If you run out of cash, the death will be quicker!*

We can only spend $1 once. Thus, we need to invest it so that the dollar gives us a greater return in a reasonable time. The two documents that help you manage cash are the budget/plan and the cash flow forecast.

*The Budget/Plan*

This is your plan. Yes, it changes over time, but, it's your focus and your goal. As an example, a pilot files a flight plan. It includes the destination, the route being flown, the amount of fuel loaded onto the aircraft, and an estimate of the flight time. Also reviewed are the terrain maps, the weather, and any midway points in case of emergency.

Once the plane is in the air, it is rarely in a straight path towards the runway at the destination. It may actually take off heading east into the wind and make a turn to head west towards the final destination, but, that's part of the plan.

The winds change, the temperature changes, the plane gets lighter as it burns off fuel, and there may be traffic. The pilot must make changes to the plan to account for all of these things. Yet, the plan always remains focused on getting safely to the final destination. Remember, you are the pilot of your career. But, for now, let's get back to budgets.

The budget is like that flight plan. The things you need to consider are slightly different for different industries, however, there are similarities in all businesses.

*It all starts with sales.*

Getting a good sales plan/budget takes skill and determination. If you ask the sales team, they have conflicts. They want to be optimistic, yet, they don't want to fall short of plan. So, the sales team tends to shoot for a lower target, making it easier for them to "succeed." Knowing this is the key to pushing them to be realistic.

If you budget sales too high, you will build a plan that you can't achieve. If you budget sales too low, you will end up strangling the company, as you will not have planned to scale up to meet the needs of your customers.

As a start up, you need to take the conservative approach and rely more on your funding sources than sales.

In an established business, look at the history of how sales team members performed. Do they fall short? Do they always exceed their goals and, more importantly, do they hold price, or drop price to close deals?

Remember, when building the sales plan, it's the margin and gross profit that counts. The dumbest person in the market often sets the price, while the smartest finds a way to show value to get a higher price or develops processes and procedures that allow them to profit at lower prices.

In one of the companies that I ran, we completely changed the way we forecasted and sold. The goal was to get a better level of predictability around our sales funnel to understand which buyers were serious and when sales would come in.

Most sales forecasts are done by having the sales team discuss the chances of closing deals, referred to as "probability weighting." Basically, they guess the likelihood of a sale closing and the time frame. It's an educated guess. They are tasked with telling you the probability, based on their personal experience, of their leads closing. You will hear a deal has an 80% chance or 20% chance of closing and the timeline. The accuracy of this process is usually very low.

Under the mindset of, "if you can't measure it, you can't manage it," I changed our sales testing process to something I refer to as "percentage completion."

We looked at all of the things that had to occur before our company actually got an order. There seemed to be a series of steps that had to happen before our customers would submit their respective orders.

First, they had to ask for a quote. Then, we would do a site survey to understand their facility. Lastly, we would submit an estimate and they would negotiate a best and final offer.

By analyzing our order life cycle, we had a better understanding of what steps needed to happen before closing a sale. Then we could say we had completed 10% of the work or 90% of the work. From there, we knew which customers were close to purchasing, and which of them needed lots more work. This helped us better understand the actions we needed to take.

By understanding this cycle, we could better predict which orders would turn into sales. We no longer guessed on percentages, we focused on understanding all the elements that must occur before the sale could be finalized. Our sales forecasting went from approximately 60% accuracy to 85%, because we better understood and analyzed the process.

As soon as we implemented this, the sales team changed their mindset and their closure rate went up, as they saw what a successful process looked like. Consequently, they became more methodical and efficient in the way they conducted business.

*How do you compensate sales people?*

Salespeople are the easiest people on the team to motivate. They are 100% coin operated. This means they are used to working for commission and they know exactly how to maximize their compensation plans.

This is both good news and bad news. Managing sales people requires that you make sure their compensation plan is in alignment with corporate needs. This starts out with making sure your sales team is focused on the right type of customer and that they are selling the products that you need them to sell. Once you are focused upon the correct customer and product, you need to take that to the next level and make sure they are selling the value and quality of the product, rather than just the price.

The best way to achieve this type of mission is to change the compensation plan to reward effective behavior. Some interesting techniques include: bonuses for new customers, giving additional commission percentages based on the margin that they sell as opposed to the price, and requiring them to sell a certain number of specific products and services that are outside the core business, but bring additional value to the company. If their bonus plan is based on the company's expectations, it will be easy to measure a sales person's effectiveness.

Now that we better understand where the sales are coming from, it's time to move on to the next major topic.

*Cash*

How to allocate cash is a true art. It is a very precious asset, as it feeds everything from product development to marketing. It pays for the lights and the rent, and of course, it funds salaries.

This balancing act has many components, and to understand them, you must ask these necessary questions.

1. How much cash do we have and how long can it last?
2. What is most important to build the company?
3. What can we get done for free?
4. What is more valuable - building the next product or monetizing the products we already have?
5. What investments will create more cash and how long will they take?
6. One of my favorite discussions that always happens: "We really need that!" My reply is always "Thou shalt not buy fancy office furniture with your first round of funding!"

I say this jokingly, however, it's true. There is a clear line between "wants" and "needs." Knowing where that line is can determine success or failure.

There are two primary needs that a company has:

1. A product/service that the market place wants and is **willing to pay for**.

2. Customers to buy those products or services.

When it comes to determining where to allocate cash, if you don't have those elements funded, everything else is irrelevant.

After products and customer acquisition, the other questions include:

- Where will you operate?

- o Once you know this, you can understand your overhead including utilities expense, what equipment you will need, and a host of other expenses.

- How do you control the costs of your products or services?
  - o Do you manufacture your products or have a 3$^{rd}$ party make them?
  - o Explore what other elements and costs are associated with getting your products out to a customer and servicing that customer. Do you make it in-house or outsource? Some examples: logistics for delivery, call center for customer service, or even a marketing agency vs. an in-house marketing people.

It's important to think and act upon these issues. It's imperative to deploy capital where you get the best return on your investments.

As part of your planning, you always need to think about the big picture. If you look at any one of those things as a standalone element, you won't understand the total cost of ownership or the amount of cash you will need to invest.

As an example, you may be able to manufacture a part for $2 and sell it for $5; that's a great mark up. If you buy that part for $3 and sell it for $5, it would appear that you are losing the opportunity to make the additional $1 in profit. This is only one part of the picture. You may have to invest $10,000 to buy the machine so that you can produce $2.00 parts. You have to ask yourself: is there anything else you could do with that $10,000 that would be more beneficial to your company's growth?

What I am asking you to do is think about that total long-term cost. If you buy a sailboat, it's not only the $200,000 spent to buy the boat that makes it costly, it's also the cost of operating it every single year that makes it so expensive. That is why it is important to look at the "total cost of ownership," the true cost. Always take a step back and look at the big picture; sometimes it is greater than the sum of the individual parts.

Why sign a long-term lease for office space, which means you also need to buy furniture and the other types of office equipment? It may be less expensive to use a shared office suite and pay a monthly fee that includes all of those items so that you do not need to purchase all of this equipment.

There are times where the exact opposite is true. I was able to lease office space that was fully furnished because the previous tenant needed to move out and I got a better deal than if I had gone to a new building and furnished it myself. My point is that nothing is as simple as it seems, and you should always look a little deeper and ask one more question to see if there's a better way to accomplish your goal.

*Customer Acquisition*

What is your customer acquisition strategy? This is one of the areas that has dramatically changed over the last few years. People only do business with us because they know us, they trust us, and they need what we have.

How do we build trust if the customer does not know us? It starts with marketing and advertising. Look at how that world has changed. The most valid source for information 25 years ago was the Yellow Pages. Some of you who are reading this book have never even seen a telephone book, much less one with yellow pages. Now there are so many digital resources, ranging from Yelp to SEO for web searches, to targeted ads running on platforms like Facebook, Instagram and LinkedIn.

Even as I write this book, the digital marketing area is changing because of the higher levels of privacy protection being implemented.

It is important not only to understand your customer acquisition strategy, but also, the best kind of customer to attract.

I propose to you that you want customers that you can build a relationship with, as opposed to customers that are simply transactional and not loyal. Transactional customers are loyal to a price, not to a source. If all of your customers are transactional, then you are constantly spending your resources (time, clock, and cash) looking for new customers. If you target customers that want to build a relationship, you have the opportunity to build a partnership. This customer will give you needed feedback, as well as sales. Accordingly, your customer acquisition strategy will have a lower lifetime cost when compared to the lifetime of value of that customer.

The most important lesson that I would like you to get from this chapter is that everything connects and it all must fit together to make it work. Look for those connection points and look for how one thing impacts another. There was a great movie made years ago titled, "The Butterfly Effect," and its premise was about how widespread the effect can be from an apparently small change. This is something that leaders and visionaries are highly aware of and continuingly work on.

## Chapter 3: The Customer Journey

User experience, user experience, user experience! I use this expression in every sense of the word "user." The user can be your customer, the user can be a potential customer, and the user can be someone you're working with who experiences you. In this chapter, we will be discussing that segment of the customer journey focused on the external customer.

From a company perspective, what's it like to be a customer? Do you make your process easy, or do you make your process difficult? These questions must be answered in order for you to have a successful career, or in order for your company to profitably **gain** and **retain** customers.

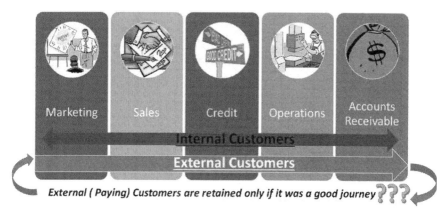

*External ( Paying) Customers are retained only if it was a good journey* ???

Let's start out with the external customer and their journey. Companies are often built in silos, meaning they have a sales department, marketing department, operations department, shipping department, and an accounting department. The people in these departments know their jobs. Often, people only focus on the elements associated with their respective department, rather than on the entirety of the customer experience.

Here's another way to think about this. Companies are built in vertical stovepipes. Customers travel horizontally through the stovepipes. The harder the walls, or the worse the communication between departments, the more difficulty a customer will face in their journey through the company.

There is an excellent Harvard Business Review article titled, *"Staple Yourself to an Order,"* written by Benson P. Shapiro, Kasturi Ragan, and John J. Sviokla. The aforementioned article takes a deep dive into the order management cycle, outlines some of the conflicts that can occur when operating businesses, and discusses how such conflicts negatively impact customers. I highly recommend you get a copy online and read it.

By stapling yourself to the order, you can actually see the internal workings of a customer experience. You should examine where things go really well and where things go horribly wrong. It's essential to highlight the various conflicts between the handoffs from department to department.

- Did the salespeople properly write up an order, such that everyone inside the company understands exactly the customer needs?
- Did anyone check the customer's credit to make sure, when an invoice is submitted, it will actually get paid? (This also would include checking the account receivable from that customer from previous sales to make sure they pay on a timely basis).
- If the customer lacks credit, who decides to ship or not ship to the customer?
- Has your team called the customer to discuss credit terms and financing? Did they approach the customer in a friendly manner or like a credit agency demanding payment?
- Did the planning team schedule the production or service delivery based on the customer's request?

- Did someone check to make sure all of the inventory was available? Did they properly schedule the purchase of materials that go into the final product?
- Was the final paperwork properly submitted to the billing department?
- Is customer service aware of the shipment and do they have the proper tracking technology, so when the customer calls to check, they can be helpful to the customer?
- If the customer is late in payment, who makes the decision to call the customer? Once again, how is the customer treated when there is a late payment?

If there is a breakdown in any one of these steps, it can increase the chances of customer dissatisfaction. A dissatisfied customer is one that the company will most likely not retain. Since our core principle is to gain and profitably retain customers, the order management cycle is critical to making sure the company does not violate that simple principle.

There are also innate conflicts of interest that need to be addressed in this order management cycle. Understanding what conflicts might occur and how to resolve these conflicts before they occur needs to be built in to your order management cycle and process.

Here are two simple examples of the type of conflicts that often occur:

- Two salespeople each have a large order. They need to be run at the exact same time in the plant in order to make the customer's deadline. The production plant does not have the capacity to run both large orders and make the deadline, so someone needs to decide which order gets done. To make it more complicated, one order is from the company's largest customer, while the other order is from a new customer that could become one of the company's largest customers in the near future. Which order gets accepted?

- o There is no easy answer to this dilemma. The main tool to resolve conflicts such as this is communication. Someone, most likely senior management rather than sales, needs to speak with each one of the customers and find out what their true needs are. Maybe one of these orders does not actually have the same urgency as the other. It's possible that one of the customers can take a smaller order to get them through, so that the company can allocate resources to both customers. This is why maintaining a good corporate relationship with customers, and not just a relationship between a particular salesperson and customer, is critically important.

- You have a customer that requires a special trucking company to deliver their product and you are obligated to book time on the customer's loading dock so that they better maintain their logistics plan. The customer has given you a specific delivery date. When your shipping department calls the customer's specified trucking company, they cannot make the pickup and deliver it to the customer on time. The contract states that they will not accept shipments from non-authorized trucking companies. Even if you do everything right, this one little element creates a problem. What do you do?

- o The obvious answer to this problem is communication. Someone needs to reach out to the customer and sort out the trucking issue or get a change in the delivery date so that their preferred carrier can be used to satisfy the customers need. While we know communication is the tool to resolve the problem, who makes the phone call? There are multiple phone calls that might need to be made. Do you call the customer and ask if they will use a different carrier or if they can change their date? If the salesperson makes the phone call because it's their customer, then who calls the trucking company to arrange the delivery? All of these elements need to be thought out in advance, so the process kicks in and the various employees throughout the company know exactly the nature of their role, and enable to company to satisfy the customer's need.

Your organization has its own set of systems and processes. By stapling yourself to the order, you can find your own conflicts and create your own resolution process. That's the power of this tool. You can anticipate problems and resolve them before they occur… and that's called leadership!

## *Chapter 4: Presence*

This chapter is dedicated to the concept of presence. So much has been written about the importance of presence, but I thought I would take a moment to give my thoughts.

Presence is the ability to be in the moment and experience exactly what is going on. Presence is "enjoying the moment" and being focused in the moment. If you are not enjoying the moment, why are you doing what you do? By the way, not every moment is easy. However, it's critical to get the most out of your moments. If you are not **present**, it's not possible enjoy the moment and see all the angles, possibilities and connections.

In today's day and age, there have been so many times that I have seen people focused on their mobile devices, glued to the screen, and foregoing eye contact while talking with me. Let's forget for the moment that this kind of behavior is just plain rude. Let's focus on the fact that not being in the moment weakens our ability to be successful.

I had a young engineer who applied to work for me a few years ago. While we were speaking, his phone began vibrating in his pocket. He asked me if he could take the call. Half of me was happy that he had the courtesy to ask, while the other half was profoundly disappointed that he lacked the common sense to: a) not turn the phone off and b) think it would be OK to take the call while trying to come work for me.

Many years ago, I read a book called, *"The Celestine Prophecy"* by James Redfield. In his book, Redfield discusses the following concept: There are no coincidences, just seized and missed opportunities. You may want to read and re-read that sentence. We've all heard the concept of "It's all out there in the universe, we just need to go for it." This is another saying that illustrates the importance of being in the moment.

I would like to share with you a story that happened to me to further prove this point. After the sale of PictureTel, I was interviewed to become the CEO of a major public company located in the Boston area. While I did not get the job, which may have been the best thing that ever happened to me, one of the board members from that company who interviewed me, asked me to visit him in his New York office. He thought there would be an opportunity that could come out of a conversation with him.

I was in his office, and we were having a nice chat when his phone rang. When he answered the phone, I had to become invisible. So, I stood up and started looking at the books in his bookshelf, because the door was closed and there was no way for me to get out to give him privacy. I was doing my best not to listen to his conversation, but he said to me as he was on the phone "Hey Lew, what do you know about the restaurant business?" I replied "Nothing." A few moments later, he asked me "Lew, can you sit on the audit committee of a public company." I replied, "Yeah, that I can do" and a few minutes later, he asked once again "Lew can you be in Miami tomorrow?" And I replied, "Sure thing."

He hung up the phone and told me he was speaking with Rocky Aoki, the founder of Benihana Corporation. He went on to tell me that Rocky was looking for a new independent board member to sit on his board. I had read the Benihana case study, kind of. That means I skimmed through it, sat with my study group, and listened to what they had to say. The next day in class, I sat as low as I could and hoped I didn't get called on. I decided not to mention that one little thing.

My point here is that, had I not accepted the invitation to New York, I would've never been in that man's office. Had he gotten the call from Rocky ten minutes before I arrived at the office or after I had left, he probably would've never thought about me.

Because I was present and honest, I was afforded the unique opportunity of flying to Florida to meet with Rocky. The rest of the story is simple. I went to the library and downloaded the Benihana case study. I read it and reread it on the flight to Florida. When I met with Rocky, every question he asked me about the restaurant industry, I answered straight out of the case study. He thought I was one of the smartest restaurant people that he had ever met.

There is a second lesson that comes out of being present, and it's called preparation. Let's go back to the unsuccessful interview which led me to the Benihana opportunity. For that meeting, I had done lots of homework about all of the people in the room and the problems that the company was having. Unfortunately, one of the board members did not fully disclose who she was in her bio, which made things difficult for me. Her grandfather had started the business and she was the family's representative on the public company board. Nowhere did it list her as a member of the family and since her last name was not the same as the founder of the company, I was unaware of the familial relationship. I was honest during the interview and shared my thoughts of how to fix the company. But in essence, they went against her grandfather's belief in the technology, which they continued to use even though it had long been outdated. Because I offended her with my honesty, she did not want me as the CEO of the company her grandfather started. I had done my homework, but clearly had not sufficiently prepared for the meeting. So, while I was present, I was unprepared for what transpired.

Within six months, the company had gone bankrupt and it appeared that my thoughts were correct. Regardless, from that moment, I got on a new journey which led me to Rocky Aoki and the opportunity to lead the board of the Benihana Corporation, perhaps one of the greatest opportunities I have ever had.

The lessons I would like you to get out of this story are those of presence and preparation. Never go into a meeting unprepared. Preparation includes understanding the topic that's going to be discussed, understanding the people sitting around the table, including their backgrounds, their perspective on the situation that you will be discussing, and any power dynamics between the people. This will allow you to truly know who you are addressing. This type of preparation is invaluable.

Proper and meticulous preparation will dramatically increase your ability to navigate any situation. Equally important, being prepared often sets you apart from others, because it is somewhat of a lost art in today's society.

As far as presence goes, if you're busy on your phone, and not cognizant of what's going on around you, how can you possibly believe that you can get the most out of the moment? There are 86,400 seconds every day. If you take out the seconds when you are sleeping, there is still plenty of time left to be focused in the moment, when the good stuff is right in front of you.

## Chapter 5: The Boss, the Manager, and the Leader

Whether your title is manager, director, vice president, CEO, or owner, you are always dealing with the concepts of leader, boss, and manager. In simple terms, my definition of each are as follows:

- **Leader**: A leader uses communication to express vision, direction and goals. Their focus is to support the team and provide the resources that drive success. Leaders leverage their interpersonal skills, otherwise known as their "emotional quotient," which is referred to as "EQ." This is the capability to recognize one's own emotions and others emotions and discern between different feelings by using emotional information to guide thinking and behavior. They manage and/or adjust emotions to adapt to their environment and achieve their goals. They heavily rely on communication skills, developing team spirit, and focusing on the morale of an organization.

- **Boss**: A boss is similar to a leader, because the boss is responsible for vision, direction, and goals. Bosses often use commands to tell people what to do, as opposed to a leader, who provides a compelling reason or attitude to motivate their team to follow.

- **Manager**: A manager is often focused on the assignment of people to specific tasks and processes. Managers are focused on making the processes better and aligning their resources, including the budget and the people around processes and procedures. In this context, the manager deals with conceptual issues in the organization, such as planning and organizing systems and procedures.

Using this overview of the three different concepts, people in a management role often flow between the three styles and focuses. The smaller the company, the more flexibility there must be to move between all three modalities. All three provide guidance, direction, and governance (a system of controls, checks, and balances of power), depending on the company's situation and needs. Any one of the three can be deployed to maximize the desired results.

The same person can be a manager and a leader; however, they serve two different purposes. As a company grows and becomes larger, it can afford to have both leaders and managers. This is when you can see how personality types come into play.

- A manager often needs to be slightly less emotionally involved and more pragmatic. They must be this way because they are reviewing what the company is doing and focused on hiring people that will be successful at getting those tasks done. Leaders tend to be more emotionally attached and intuitive.

- It's easy to train a manager. They can learn the tasks that need to be accomplished and execute because they have a skill set that includes logic and a practical personality type. Leaders, on the other hand, are harder to find because they often have to have an innate skill set and belief in what they're doing to get the most out of a team. They need to be comfortable putting themselves last and spending significant emotional energy on selling their ideas and vision, while motivating the team.

- Managers help their organization deal with complexity by creating systems. Leaders inspire the organization and help it adapt to change.

- Managers organize people around a set of tasks, while leaders align people around a common vision.

- Managers use control techniques to get things accomplished, while leaders are most often employing motivational techniques.

There are three styles of leadership: Authoritarian, Participative, and Delegative. Each respective style has significant benefits and drawbacks. Great leaders slide easily between all three styles. They instinctively know when each style will be the most effective.

- **Authoritarian (Autocratic)**: This style is often most effective in an early stage company for which time and resources are so critical the leader has very few managers in the organization and is balancing so many items that there is limited time for discussion and debate. This type of leader has no margin for error, so they must know their business and what needs to get accomplished.
    o Pros: This is a style that tells people what to do and may or may not tell people why they're doing it. It keeps people on task and focused on a goal.
    o Cons: Autocrats do not take advice or feedback from others. They're often in the mindset of "my way or the highway."

- **Participative (Democratic)**: This type of leader uses the organization to give feedback and make suggestions on necessary improvements. This is a more typical style once a company leaves startup mode and moves into an early stage state.

  o Pros: Managers inside an organization who lead it in a democratic fashion are given the opportunity to lead their individual organizations and participate in both major and minor decisions. This style gets the best ideas on the table and is not dependent on any single person's thought process to drive success.

  o Cons: Democratically run organizations often lose their nimbleness, because so many people are part of the decision-making process. With so many different ideas in play at the same time, they often suffer from analysis paralysis, because everyone is so driven to get it right; they're often slow to act.

- **Delegative (Free Reign)**: This style empowers the entire organization to do what it needs to do in order to achieve maximum results. The leader communicates the vision and then counts on the team to get things done.

  o Pros: When an organization is empowered, job satisfaction goes up, along with creativity and departmental effectiveness. Things get done more quickly, because there are fewer decision-makers in the day-to-day activities.

  o Cons: When an organization is empowered, and the leader is not highly involved, it allows for fiefdoms or silos of power to be created. Each department is working in its best interest; however, it may be not in the best interest of the organization as a whole.

The tools leaders and managers use also include command and control. Command guides the organization using a well thought out vision, communicates it throughout the organization, and then sees to the effectiveness in that organization. Control provides structure to the organization to make it efficient and effective.

There is a delicate balancing act that leaders and managers need to follow. They both have to have a level of concern for people and tasks. If there is a low concern for people and tasks in the organization, the organization will be impoverished and is destined to fail. If there is a limited concern for people, but a great concern for tasks, the corporate culture can become authoritarian and toxic. When the management is more concerned with the people, with a limited focus on the tasks, it often becomes a fun and social place to work, yet it also becomes inefficient, ineffective, and ultimately a failure. When leaders and managers work together to be concerned for both the people and the tasks at a high level, the corporate culture is one of teamwork and quality. In theory, this would be the ideal balance. However, this last scenario, leaders and managers can burn out their team. If the concern is very high about the people and the tasks simultaneously, everything becomes important. By definition, if everything is important, then nothing has importance, and it can end up creating confusion throughout the organization.

The words efficient and effective are dramatically different, yet inextricably linked. Efficient is getting the most throughput while effective adds quality to the efficiency.

An example might be a company with a maximum production capacity of 1000 widgets per day. Perhaps they're able to produce 1100 widgets in a day, which means they were incredibly efficient. If the rejection rate based on quality is high, and they have to throw out a significant number of their widgets, that organization, while being efficient in their production capacity, is highly ineffective, because of the reject rate.

One of my favorite of the Murphy's Laws is, "There's never enough time to do it right, but there's always enough time to do it twice." Effective organizations plan appropriately and build quality into everything they do. This often takes additional time and resources at the front end of any project, but it dramatically reduces the amount of rework or waste. That is the only way to avoid the trap of this Murphy's Law.

I've developed a list of what I refer to as the attributes of an entrepreneur and an intrapreneur, which tie directly into the concepts of great leaders, bosses, managers, and owners. I have segmented these attributes and suggest you take a personal inventory of the ones you have and the ones you need to develop. I've divided them into categories - personal and professional attributes. Many of these attributes belong in both columns.

| Professional | Personal |
|---|---|
| Resourceful | Honest |
| Self-reliant | Empathetic |
| Persistent | Active listener |
| Risk taker | Compassionate |
| Adaptive | Tolerant |
| Reactive | Wise |
| Persuasive | Courageous |

Just being aware of these attributes is the first step toward behaving like a CEO or a leader. These are mindsets; some you are born with, and others you learn. It is like muscle memory. If you are aware of them and you practice them, they will become second nature.

Leaders understand the importance of everyone's time, not just their own. They also have the unique ability to understand the difference between important and urgent. Stephen Covey, entrepreneur and author of his book, *"The 7 Habits of Highly*

*Successful People,"* discusses the importance of knowing these differences and how to enlist help as being one of the key drivers to a successful career.

He developed a mindset tool on how to make decisions and who should make those decisions. He called it his "Prioritization Matrix." He considers both what is important and urgent and then puts them in this matrix, shown below.

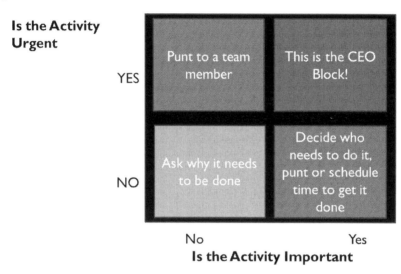

Using this tool will add time to your day for what is important. The goal is to drive success by having the right people do the right things at the right time, making everyone more productive.

## Chapter 6: Keeping Track of the Important Stuff

"If you can't measure it, you can't manage it."

To lead a successful team, organization, or company, measurement of performance is key! You must know the crucial combination of measurement and management to drive your career forward. It is critically important to combine where you are with where you are going. It's equally important to know where you are along the way and how every element of your plan and your team is performing on the journey.

Parsing that sentence, "If you can't measure it, you can't manage it," into halves, the first half speaks to the importance of management and what is truly critical to measure, both of which we will be discussing in this chapter. The second half discusses management of what's important.

You may often hear these acronyms: KPI (key performance indicators) and CSF (critical success factors). These two concepts are inextricably linked. The CSFs are concepts, initiatives, and behaviors that support and advance your strategy. The KPIs are the ways to measure the success of your strategy and vision.

The first and most important critical CSF is you. As a leader or manager, you start the process. It's interesting when you think about leadership and power; the actual power starts with the first follower. If no one is following you, are you a leader? The true power that a leader has is the power of communication. You can give people a compelling reason to follow, a type of leadership that is often highly effective. You could also boss people around and tell them what they have to do using your title or position in the company as a hammer to force people to get things done. Sadly, both things work, but the best type of leader inspires others to go above and beyond, putting them in a position where they want to come to work. A boss, on the other hand, gets people to do things, but often in a sloppy fashion. As a result, those employees are probably looking for work elsewhere.

For every critical success factor, there is also an associated key performance indicator. If you are providing ineffectual leadership, one KPI might be employee turnover. Why is this important? Every time someone leaves, there is an expense associated with recruiting someone new, training them, the early mistakes that they make prior to training, etc. Going back to the 7Cs, this often has a dramatic impact on cash and customers, both internal and external.

Managing your CSF is the first step in advancing your career and becoming more valuable and more effective in your position.

Some other CSFs are not necessarily measurable, but they can be highly visible in either a good way or a bad way. These are concepts such as integrity, quality, passion, and style of leadership.

As the leader, you are always being judged. It is important to remember, which is why I repeat this numerous times in this book, **"How others experience you is your brand."**

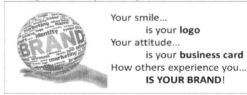

Your smile...
is your **logo**
Your attitude...
is your **business card**
How others experience you...
**IS YOUR BRAND**!

Sometimes you must ask yourself: How do your team members and subordinates see you? Not only what they are judging, but also, is what they see in alignment with how you see yourself? If there is no alignment, what does that say about you? This self-discovery process is one that every great leader goes through, as their style and the culture that they drive evolves over time.

The decision to follow is often made from these intangibles. Ask yourself, "What do I see in the leaders that I choose to follow?" You will soon get a better understanding of this concept. Do you follow people that yell at you for no reason, or even those that yell at you for something reasonable, rather than communicating in a civil fashion? Do you follow people that tell you to do things, or would you rather follow someone that explains to you why you're doing it, or paints the big picture from time to time?

Some other personal CSFs are ego, stomach, and energy. Can you truly put your ego aside? I have often dealt with engineers who believe so strongly in themselves that they adopt "the not invented here" mentality. They are so blinded by their own excellence that they forget that there are other excellent engineers in other places. It can cost a great deal of resources to develop something that you may be able to buy from a third-party at a lower cost, saving cash and time (clock). Can you be open-minded enough to not let your ego drive decisions?

In the early days of personal computing, before Apple released its groundbreaking PC named "Lisa," Steve Jobs was focused on making the use of computers much easier. Job's vision was based on something he called "WYSIWYG" which stood for "what you see is what you get." At that time, what you would see on a computer screen was all the commands mixed into a sentence. The font, type size and spacing would be a string of code. When you actually saw something printed, it looked dramatically different.

Jobs was focused on making the screen and the printed product look identical.

As part of this pursuit, he also wanted an easier way to interact with the computer. He knew the keyboard was critical, but entering commands was cumbersome and rarely intuitive. He had his team looking at easier ways to accomplish these tasks.

Jobs visited Xerox's Palo Alto Research Campus (PARC) where he saw the mouse for the first time. This was nothing like the interfaces that they were looking at Apple. He decided that this mouse and user interface was better and easier. They stopped the development at Apple on their internal ideas and switched over to what Jobs had seen at Xerox.

The acceptance that someone, even a competitor, is doing something better than you, can lead to great things. The mouse is one of those amazing examples of avoiding the "not invented here syndrome."

I call this open-mindedness being **passionately dispassionate**. I realize those words seem to contradict each other, but that's not the case. By behaving in a passionately dispassionate way while you're examining options, the ego is inherently taken out of the equation. A leadership role, when fully functioning, is one that elicits great ideas from the team, and then demonstrates the wisdom to pick the right one. If the leader is always focused on being right, there are no options left for the rest of the team to contribute or excel. Again, put yourself in their shoes; do you want to be at a place where your creativity and excellence is ignored and negated? Or, do you want to be in a place where you get to not only work in your genius, but also to contribute to the greater good of the organization. Once again, it gets down to the concept of one of our Cs - cooperation.

Another personal critical success factor is this: do you have the stomach to do what it takes? Entrepreneurs in early-stage companies often are challenged whether or not they can make payroll on Friday. That is an incredible amount of stress and pressure, which is then compounded by the implications for their personal lives. Are you ready to manage that level of stress or anxiety? I'm not telling you that every day you will have that level of stress, but, if you do not have the stomach for stress, as well as the loneliness at the top, it can break you if you're ill prepared.

Expanding on "loneliness at the top," there are times when you must separate yourself from the team. Unfortunately, one of the realities of life is that people often look for flaws. As the leader, you can't share your flaws, you can't share too much about your personal life, and as an attorney once said to me, "never give the enemy the ammunition to shoot you." I am not saying your team members are your enemy, however, they are often the people on the other side of the table. Whenever we are negotiating for something, we all use points of leverage, and it does you no good as a leader to give up points of leverage that someone may choose to use inappropriately. I would like to think everyone stays professional all the time. The truth of the matter is, as a leader, you must. But, this does not guarantee that your team will, always behave in the same fashion.

It is also lonely when you're at the top of an organization because many people come to you and share only a portion of their agenda. Often, there can be a hidden agenda at play. While this is very frustrating, it's a reality of life. Thus, not only do you have to have the stomach for listening for the cues, but also, you need to find a way to manage around the hidden agenda or through it. The simplest examples are when someone needs additional time off. Employees will often make up stories, leaving you to decipher how much of what they told you is truth. Some people will come to your office and behave in a passive aggressive fashion, leaving you to think through what's really going on.

The guidance that I can give you is one of active listening, combined with situational awareness. As a leader, you are also a juggler. You need to know what's going on in your organization, as well as a vast majority of both the factual situations and the political situations. Organizations are made up of people. As a result, they can often be unpredictable because we all bring our perspectives along with us. With active listening, you can ask good questions and look for inconsistencies in a story that you're being told. These potential inconsistencies can also tell you a story. Situational awareness puts the story in the context of the bigger picture. When you marry the stories that you're hearing to the big picture, you can often get to the truth, or what we call in engineering, the *root cause*. Think of *root cause* as the first domino in a line of dominoes to fall. When you can find the root, where things began, you can truly understand the situation and make the most pragmatic decisions.

The next critical success factor is that of patience and personality. Do you have the patience to comprehend and analyze people's stories? Are you prepared to listen to multiple ideas as to how to solve a problem? Do you do what is necessary to juggle multiple communication styles from various team members? The answer here does not necessarily need to be "YES" 100% of the time. However, it can never be "NO" 100% of the time. Unless you are a sole practitioner at what you do, a significant part of your role is to motivate people. That means you have to speak multiple languages when it comes to communication style. You need to have the patience to listen to someone who may speak slowly, repeat themselves, or ramble. Staying engaged and truly listening is crucial for them to believe you are able to hear what they had to say.

Patience is necessary for gaining information from others and important to give yourself a moment to pause and reflect on what is going on. Then you need to move into personality, as that is how your team will see your reactions. If your personality is knee-jerk or yelling, you have to ask yourself, why would people open up to you, support you, or help you achieve your goals?

In addition, you must incorporate a teacher's mentality into your personality. As a manager or a leader, you often are "in the loop" about most situations that are going on in the company. Your role, as you are inspiring others, is also to teach them and accept that part of teaching is questioning. While I may have the title "professor" when on campus, being a professor is relatively easy, as you simply share useful information with students. However, I don't find out if I'm a teacher until the end of the semester, when I can really see that my students have learned. Teaching is actually a higher calling than just being a professor. The same is true in management. If you profess, or tell people ideas and insist they do them, it doesn't mean they understand why they're doing it. It doesn't mean that they are on a mission, and it doesn't mean they sustain their effort when not in your presence. If you take a teacher's mindset and you make sure your team learns, and you teach your team to think on their own as if they were the boss and focused on a mission, then you have done a great service for the company and for your team.

The key performance indicators that are associated with the critical success factors of leadership can only be measured indirectly. These indicators include employee retention, employee job satisfaction, and most importantly, profitability of your department or organization.

There are also critical success factors for your business. To start off, let's discuss the structure of your organization. Is the organization designed to be nimble and reactive to both internal demands and external expectations? Is your company a customer driven organization?

The concept of a customer driven organization is a company for which the processes and procedures are designed around the most effective way to meet the customers' needs. It is one that is designed to deliver a quality product, while simultaneously being operationally effective and efficient.

This means that you think about all customer interactions with the organization, as well as the organization's interactions with in itself.

When looking internally, are the people in the organization structured in a fashion that is both efficient and effective, while focusing on profits, quality, and sustainability?

There must be an emphasis on the CFS of market awareness and focus. Notice that I separated the two concepts. Market awareness is the understanding of the ecosystem in the market or markets that you are approaching. This includes your competitor's approach to the marketplace, the pricing in the marketplace, and shifts in both customer behavior and market desire for your goods and services. When one understands these factors, clarity of focus is obtained. You can then answer the questions: Where do I muster resources? What is the best way to communicate to the market? Most importantly, is this a market in which my company should be competing?

Core competence! The core competence of an organization is at the heart of the CSF ecosystem. A company's core competence is something that is hard to duplicate and makes the organization importantly different. A core competence might be innovation, technical proficiency, marketing, product design, or the ability to integrate existing products and services, and repackage them in a way that excites consumers in the marketplace.

A great example of a company that truly understands its core competence is Honda Motor Company. Their core competence is in the name of the business. Honda doesn't make windshield wipers or tires, they don't manufacture taillight plastic or light bulbs. They have an excellence and competence around integrating all those components around the motor.

They make everything from motorcycles to cars, from jet engines to robots that use electric motors. This does not discount their ability to be amazing marketers; they understand the logistics of moving finished products on a global scale.

An underrated core competence is integration. There is incredible power in this core competency. Sometimes, I refer to this type of company as a chocolate cake company. There has always been chocolate, sugar, flour, eggs, and water. Some people make a chocolate cake that is amazing using these ingredients, while others make something closer to a chocolate brick. Knowing how to integrate the ingredients is a huge competence.

A great example of this might be Apple. They never invented the hard drive, the processing chip, or touchscreen glass. However, their wisdom to instead integrate all these elements has built the most valuable company in the world. While no one can say that Apple does not have an egotistical corporate culture, they don't let the "not invented here" syndrome impact their product development or introduction of great products into the marketplace.

The key performance indicators that can help you understand the alignment of the organization, also measure the effectiveness of each interaction point.

When designing the key performance indicators, it is important to remember the difference between important and interesting. A simple example might be it's interesting to know how many active customers you have. It is important to know how your customers are growing. Do they continue to do business with you on a regular basis? Are they referring your business and are you balancing the growth of your business by bringing on new customers? Every business selects its own key performance indicators. However, since "all business are the same, they are designed to gain and retain customers profitably in order to create value," we can think of KPIs that may be fine-tuned for an individual business. Regardless, they measure similar things that all successful companies should be analyzing as they manage their performance.

## Corporate KPIs

The financial key performance indicators are reasonably standard. The definitions, while important, are not nearly as important as what they can tell you about a business.

**Gross Margin**: A percentage based on total sales minus the cost of goods sold.

> Understanding the gross margin gives important information about the relationship between the cost of the product and what you are selling the product for in the marketplace. It can help a company to understand market dynamics and pressures regarding pricing, as well as the relationship between what it costs to make a product or deliver a service relative to how the marketplace values that product, and how your competitors behave in the marketplace, as well.

**Sales Growth:** This KPI is usually tracked quarter-over-quarter or year-over-year.

There are sub elements to sales growth. How much of the sales growth might be from a price increase? What is the ratio of existing customers to new customers? What is the concentration of your sales? In other words, do you have a broad base of customers? Does all of your business come from one place?

The importance of knowing where your sales are coming from cannot be overstated. Having multiple KPIs, as listed above, will help drive strategy going forward. If you're not adding new customers, you are at risk of losing revenue. If any one customer gets too big, you risk losing account control and potentially cash flow if your customer runs into economic hardships.

**Customer Acquisition Cost:** The costs of identifying and attracting customers. This includes the cost of generating a lead, but more importantly, the cost of attracting a paying customer.

There are so many elements that go into this measurement. Where are you finding your customers? How much do you have to invest to get one? What does it take to go from a lead to an actual customer? Clearly, customer is one of my favorite "C" words. It's critical to measure everything around the customer, from where you find them, to how you manage them, and ultimately, how satisfied are they? Measuring customer acquisition costs will help you focus on increasing customer profitability, as you will target buying customers, better understanding the messaging that attracts customers and fine-tuning your customer offerings.

**Pipeline:** Pursuing both qualified and unqualified leads, and understanding that they have different closing percentages, is important. An inflow of unqualified leads shows that your marketing is working because you are attracting new people that you don't know. It is not a bad idea to track your marketing spend to an increase in unqualified leads.

In order to predict future success, it is critical to have a robust pipeline. The percentage of potential new customers in your pipeline may never come to fruition, which is why including a measurement around success rate is important. They should also be measured salesperson by salesperson, rather than as a collective group measurement.

**Profitability by Customer:** The name of this KPI speaks for itself. It is more complicated than it sounds. Some customers require significant resources just to close a sale. Other customers demand better pricing, which, as a result, lowers your margins.

Understanding how each customer impacts your business is critical. There is an old saying: "Price, service, terms - a customer gets to pick two out of the three." Measuring the value of each customer gives a company the opportunity to see where they're making and losing money.

Knowing customer profitability actually gives the organization the ability to fire a customer. This is one of the hardest things to do, because we often chase the Holy Grail of topline revenue.

At PictureTel, we had a customer who kept driving a hard bargain and threatening to leave us for a competitor. I had my sales team review the cost of this customer; we lost money on every system we shipped. It was clear it would've been cheaper to give the customer the $1,000 per system they ordered, then to ship a system to them. Having this knowledge gave us leverage to go back to the customer and give them the option of renegotiating the nature of our relationship or have them help our competitors lose $1,000 per system.

**Profitability by Product Line:** Know the cost of each product and its relative impact on revenue. This would be total cost, which includes not only the cost of the product when you put it into inventory, but also, how long it sits on a shelf. It is important to note that there is also the cost of capital and opportunity cost associated with every product.

> Knowing the relative value of every product in your inventory or service offering gives you the opportunity for the occasional housekeeping. Sometimes this drives SKU (Stock Keeping Unit) rationalization - if your company is offering too many selections or, as a product slows down, you can manage the product's lifecycle or establish a product refresh in order to reinvigorate the revenue potential. This is also important information because you can see if and when one product is cannibalizing the revenue of another, and if you should be carrying both. Lastly, slow-moving products tie up an incredibly valuable resource, CASH.

**Average Conversion Time:** This measures the time it takes from the first sales call until an order is taken. There also needs to be a measurement that details the time between when an order is taken and delivered, relative to the time originally promised to the customer.

> In order to predict the sales pipeline and funnel, it's critical to know how long orders take to go from the quote stage all the way until the order is taken. If there is a long lead time required for a certain product line, it will require greater planning and cash management for the cycle time until the order becomes real. This also means the sales team must have a much larger pipeline to allow for some deals to fall out and other deals to close.

I am also including in this section the conversion time associated to the date a customer is expecting their order, as opposed to the date the company actually delivers. This can drive a customer satisfaction score and can also highlight the salespersons' aggressive nature to accept what the company cannot deliver, and thus, fail to meet customers' expectations.

**Planned Cost vs. Actual Cost**: This measurement drives the difference between budget and experienced costs, which both impact planning and quoting.

This critical measurement highlights the effectiveness of the internal organization's ability to deliver a quality product against the plan. It's a way to measure multiple elements inside your manufacturing or product development organizations. Does the company really know its costs? Is there significant rework because the company has a very high waste component? Over time, this will impact a companies' sustainability.

**Return on Investment (ROI)**: The yield based on the use of cash against any given investment. This can be used to measure any use of cash. The purchase of equipment, the purchase of advertising, or investments in a potential customer before an order is received.

ROI ultimately determines the effectiveness of a company's use of cash. While it can be used to measure almost any investment, it also needs to be compared against opportunity cost. If any investment is yielding too low of a return, this problem is compounded by having not explored other opportunities that may have had a higher yield.

This is not an exhaustive list of key performance indicators. My goal is to give you some measurements and get you to think about other measurements that can drive your company forward. There is a dramatic difference between data and information. That is the same thing with KPIs. You must be aware and recognize the correct measurements, the ones that tell the real story. The goal is to understand the things you're measuring and how they impact your customers, and potentially your profitability.

Another word that is repeated often in this book is ecosystem. Ultimately, everything is connected in a larger ecosystem. There is a strategy that your company is using to drive towards achieving its goals. In order to have success, you need to measure both what's going well and what's not going well. Therefore, you have key performance indicators. Taking the key performance indicators and understanding the impact of each respective indicator will allow you to better understand your critical success factors.

This chapter started out with the quote, "If you can't measure it, you can't manage it." It also began with the leadership concept of "inspect what you expect." The last critical success factor included in this chapter focuses on having the ability to select the right measurements that are in alignment with both the company's mission and desire in the marketplace.

When you put all of these things together, you are left with two decisions or action steps: motivate or terminate! Leaders either make things better, which is motivate, or they make a decision to go in another direction, which is terminate. Ultimately, it's your choice

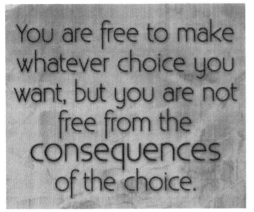

You are free to make whatever choice you want, but you are not free from the consequences of the choice.

In the early 1990s, we purchased a building to house our company. The building was over 100 years old. It was in the national register for historic buildings and was originally designed as a manufacturing facility for making baby shoes.

There was an elevator in the center of the building, which was designed more than a century ago and clearly not safe. There was a cable going from the third floor, down to the basement. The operator would stick an arm out of a small window in the elevator car and pull the cable up to go up, and down to go down. The state of Massachusetts had banned this type of elevator over 10 years earlier. We were told we needed to replace it with a safer, more modern elevator in order to get our occupancy permits.

The elevator was in the middle of the building and it would've been impossible to replace it. We made the decision to build an elevator shaft outside of the building and then just cut holes in the side of the building for the doors. The first thing we needed to do was drill a hole for a piston for floors below ground, in order to lift the new elevator car up and down. As we started to drill, we were required to test the dirt underneath the building by law. We soon found out that what they used to make baby shoes white was a chemical element named barium, a cancer-causing material. It was our responsibility to clean up the dirt, which practically tripled the cost of building the elevator. The important life lesson here was it's the things that are underground that you don't see that can get you in a lot of trouble. This is why, to this day, I make lists of all the things I need to accomplish, which often include things that appear trivial. But, they can become incredibly important when not dealt with in a timely fashion.

**Words and phrases that I hate!**

**"If"** is a prime example. "Balls, said the Queen, **if** I had them, I'd be King."

**If** is an incredibly powerful word, but it often leads to no good. When we focus on what is not happening, we are putting into the universe the concept of something that is negative. Keeping a positive mindset is critical to staying motivated and making great things happen. Often, the two words "if" and "only" go together. Throughout my life, I have heard people say, "if only I did this" or "if only that happened." While this is wishful thinking, it has no value in the world of entrepreneurship. You make things happen or you don't; it's a binary decision that **if** plays no part in making.

**"Maybe"** is such a passive word. What makes entrepreneurs successful is commitment. "Maybe" is wishy-washy, and allows for both "I will" or "I won't" simultaneously. It's almost like Schrödinger's cat; it is both alive and dead at the same time. While that works in quantum physics, in the business world, "maybe" is the word used when people try to avoid things. How often have you used the word "maybe" because you really don't want to do something, but you want to keep your options open for a backup plan? More often than not, "maybe" turns to a "no." As an entrepreneur or an intrapreneur, you should always commit to do something. If it can't happen, it's okay to change, but by showing commitment to your team, your customers, and even your investors, they will in turn have an easier time believing and following you.

**"Try"** is another word that is overused and represents the avoidance of true commitment. The second you say, "I will try to get that done," you've already built in your excuse because when things don't happen, you can always put your hands up in the air and say, "Well, at least I tried." Not dissimilar to the word "maybe," "try" distances you from actually getting things accomplished. It is much more powerful to say, "I will do it" or "I won't do it." It's a direct form of communication. The more you add complexity or allow for confusion, the harder it is to get things done.

**"Fault!"** This is a word for the ages. It's often heard in one of two sentences: "It's not my fault" or "It's their fault." Either way, it is the ultimate avoidance of accepting responsibility and taking ownership of an action. Have you ever been in a situation in which blaming someone or avoiding responsibility actually ended with a great result? I am guessing the answer to that question is, "No." We've all heard the expression, "When you point a finger at someone, three fingers are pointing back at you." Again, what difference does that make? When anything happens, share the successes and learn from the failures. Blaming someone or not taking responsibility/accountability never advances the ball. When something goes wrong, the key priority is to learn from it. Make a plan, and then execute to make sure that the same mistake never happens again. Murphy's Law kicks in at that moment; it always seems to be true that there's never enough time to get it right, but there's always enough time to do it twice. If you learn from your mistakes, it will lower the number of times you do things twice, which will, as a result, always increase **cash,** one of my favorite "C" words.

## Simple Rules

### *The French Fry Rule*

In life, there are things we know we just shouldn't do. This is true in business as well. The truth is, once we do one of those questionable things once, it is easier to do them again, and again.

That's why I say never compromise your integrity. Once you've lost it, you may make bad compromises again and again. Even if others don't know you gave up your integrity, you do, and that's all that really counts. What compounds this problem, you will have great justifications each time to make yourself feel better.

My father used to tell my brother and I all of the time, "They can take everything away from you, but your word of honor, that's yours to give."

Here's when the French Fry Rule takes over. I developed this rule when I bought my first new car. I swore to myself I would never, ever, eat in the car. I knew that was my only option if I wanted to keep it clean and smelling great.

Needless to say, one day, while on a long commute, I had a breakdown in discipline and decided to buy some fries. I'm sure you know where this story is going. I dropped a French Fry between my seat in the center console. You know the spot, it's where you can never reach, *ever*.

After that day, all hell broke loose. Coffee came into the car, the occasional breakfast sandwich, and yes, more French fries, some for me, and some to add to the collection between the seat and the console.

My point here is that if I had never had that first French fry, I would never have to worry about all of the others. If you know something is wrong, then just do the right thing.

Another way of looking at the French Fry Rule is discipline. We've all heard that successful people make their beds every day. It becomes a habit and starts off your day by accomplishing a task. The discipline of habit creates sustainability and repeatability. The French Fry Rule is nothing more than discipline.

## *The Choice Rule*

I hate to break the news to you, but everything you do is a choice. When you're late, it's a choice. I know that can seem to be upsetting because you had no intention of being late, however, you chose what time to leave for a meeting. Consequently, whatever you're doing in advance of leaving for that meeting was more important than being on time for the meeting itself. You consciously chose to do something that was more important.

You turned in something that was not your best work. Ask yourself, is that because there were other things that were more important, and you thought that you could get away with a lower quality product and no one would notice? Here again, that was your choice!

Understanding this simple point will help you take ownership of your decisions and your actions. This is an underpinning of being seen as a great leader. We've all heard that there are people that talk the talk, but don't walk the walk. Those are the type of people that don't accept the consequences of their choices. Those are the type of people that keep their options open to say it wasn't my fault. We all know that's not true, because our choices and decisions actually define who we truly are. When you adopt the entrepreneurial mindset, this includes knowing that everything you do is a choice; everything has trade-offs. You have to be quick, yet thoughtful, in order to make the right decision in the right amount of time. This is a skill, and the more you practice it, the better you will get at decision-making, and the closer you well get to being successful.

### Just Another F- -king Initiative

Change. The only constant is change. It is important for both the leader and an organization to be flexible and to embrace change. There is a fine line here, because team members often react to a change coming down from leadership as just *another f- -king initiative*. They don't take things seriously if you keep changing in a big way, rather than in increments. When that happens, they keep their head down knowing that in a few days there will be another change. Eventually, things change so much that nothing becomes status quo, and no positive change occurs.

This behavior actually has a negative impact on corporate culture. In my experience, there are a couple times in a year when major initiatives can have the largest impact because people are expecting change. Those days are New Year's, at the beginning of a new quarter, and for those in the US - Memorial Day and Labor Day. People expect change at the end of the school year and the beginning of the school year, they've had that all their lives and this expectation carries into the workplace. These dates are the ideal time to make major changes and initiatives. While I consistently say it's important to embrace change, too many changes too quickly add to corporate confusion and result in poor internal communications. For large organizations, it's hard to get everyone on the same version of an initiative in a very short period of time.

This is a great example of where communication and consistency are so important. Sharing the initiative, including why it is important and how it will improve the organization is something that people impacted want to know. Not providing this type of information allows for resistance or avoidance.

## *The Customer is Always Right*

We have all heard this from the beginning of time - the customer is *always* right. On some level, this is correct. Truth is, the customer always needs to be treated as if he or she is right, exemplified by active listening, common courtesy, and respect. This does not mean the customer was right, or that you will need to deliver exactly what they are looking for in order to satisfy them.

It's important that people who are "customer facing," representing the company to the public, also have the tools, training and authority to protect the company, while, at the same time, protecting the customer relationship. These "customer facing" people need to have the authority and flexibility to do the right thing for the right reasons. Sadly, they often don't have either. This lack of flexibility often leads to people putting policy and procedure over customers. I am not saying that there is no reason that internal processes and procedures have been implemented, but they need to be reviewed and there needs to be an understanding that customer relations and situations cannot always be handled in an "one size fits all" approach.

Team members that have no control over the destiny of customer interaction will only get heated themselves. This often leads to a dissatisfied customer and a very unhappy team member. The more you empower the team to help customers while still protecting the company, the higher the job satisfaction, and the higher the customer satisfaction.

I recently had a problem with a cell phone overheating. My warranty had expired, and my carrier told me to call the manufacturer. It was clearly not only a defect, but potentially a dangerous situation.

While I was frustrated with the carrier, the person that I spoke with made the effort to make phone calls to supervisors to see if there was anything that they could do for me. They found a bulletin from the manufacturer saying that this was a known problem and that they had a replacement program in place for this specific manufacturing defect. But, I would have to deal directly with the manufacturer. This was helpful, even if they could not help me resolve the problem, they gave me a direction and hope.

I called the 1-800 number as I was told to do, and after speaking to four different people that had no idea what I was talking about, I finally got a supervisor that was very well aware of the situation.

This supervisor was more than willing to help me based on their processes and procedures. I was told if I send back my phone, I would get a free replacement telephone within ten days. As the customer, I made what I believed to be a compelling argument that this was a manufacturer's defect and that the only communication device that I had was this cell phone. I explained to them that I could not go without connectivity for 10 days and operate my business, stay in touch with my family, and be available for emergency situations.

The supervisor listened to my compelling argument and then proceeded to say, "sorry sir, but that's the protocol." He told me that he had no discretion and there was no one above him that could change this decision. He told me he could send an email to another department and see if there was someone else that could help me.

I asked for the email address so that I could follow up directly or, better yet, a telephone number at which time the person with whom I was speaking told me he's not allowed to give out that information. Not only did they not treat me right, but also, they did not even give me the opportunity to talk to someone in the organization that might have the ability to remediate what was clearly a safety issue.

I will never buy from that manufacturer again, and I will tell everyone I know this story of poor service and process trumping customers' needs. The service department, through their inflexibility, reduced the "total life time value" of a customer and most likely lost other potential customers as I share this story.

This story is another example of the importance of seeing the big picture.

I believe my situation is unique because, in this case, the customer was right. The bigger issue that I'm highlighting is that at no point did anyone actually try to think through the problem or acknowledge the problem, they only told me about their process.

Some companies bend over backwards. There are numerous stories about Nordstrom's taking products back, when the product wasn't even purchased at Nordstrom's. They go above and beyond to satisfy a customer, because they understand the importance of making customers feel wanted; it's part of their ethos.

I once heard Tony Hsieh, the CEO of Zappos and best-selling author of *"Delivering happiness a path to profits passion and purpose,"* speak at a conference. He told a story in which someone called into Zappos. When the customer service person asked, "Is there anything else we can do for you?" after that customer placed an order, the customer replied, "You can send me a pizza." The customer service rep took his address and actually had a pizza sent to the customer. That is one way to exceed a customer's expectations.

In the previous chapter, I discussed that it's *okay* to fire a customer. This may contradict the title of this section of the book, however, if you are losing money on a customer and his or her demands are unreasonable, you should explain, in the politest possible way, that your company is no longer in a position to take care of them in a way that they desire. You would be acknowledging the customers' needs, but at the same time, you would also be honoring your company's needs, as well.

### *No Surprises in a Public Setting*

A very powerful tool that you can start employing immediately is the concept of "the meeting before the meeting." There is nothing worse than sitting in a meeting and having someone drop a bomb and then walk out of the room. This gives no one time to think and have the ability to respond in a cogent manner.

Have meetings before the meeting. Pick up the phone and talk to the attendees before you meet together and discuss this new information. Give people time to think it through so they can respond in an intelligent fashion. This will also give you the opportunity to work on building a trusting relationship and get feedback, so that you are not surprised by anything that occurs in that meeting.

Building consensus within an organization is strength, not a vulnerability. Whether you are a boss or a leader, you need to focus on getting things done. Helping people come along for the ride is the way better approach. You can also flesh out your ideas with some fine-tuning.

The bottom line here is that using "the meeting before the meeting" and avoiding public surprises builds trust and allows you the opportunity to learn more about what your team is thinking. Doing this may give you a kernel of information that you didn't have before, and may help you to be even more successful.

# *Chapter 8: Relationships*

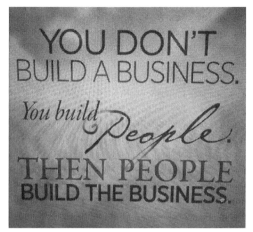

There has never been a business created that does not rely on key relationships. The relationship between a company and its customers, the relationship between a company and its vendors, and, of course, the relationship between the team members, cannot be overstated.

The opening paragraph in this chapter actually contains multiple mistakes. While it's okay to categorize a relationship between a company and people, the truth is that relationships are **always between people**. This gets back to the concept of, "how others perceive you is your brand" and the importance of communication, another one of my favorite "C" words.

In any relationship, what you say is way less important than what is heard or perceived. This puts the onus of communication on the person who is delivering the message. Speaking French to a Spaniard is not the best way to deliver a message. It is critical to deliver the message in a fashion that "the person on the other side of the table" can comprehend and act upon.

There are specific tools to help you understand other people, including the Myers-Briggs analysis and the Predictive Index. I strongly suggest you go online and learn more about these two wonderful tools.

We rarely have the opportunity to use these tools with our vendors or customers. However, they are great tools to use internally with your team members. Understanding the core principles behind Myers-Briggs will help you see some of these traits in people that you did not test.

The results of the Myers-Briggs analysis creates an opportunity to better understand the person on the other side of the table. Just understanding the concepts that the Myers-Briggs explores will dramatically improve your communication with other people, regardless of whether you actually know their test results.

Myers-Briggs simplifies the understanding of people's behavior into four major categories. They are "where you get your energy/motivation," "your most natural way of understanding information," "the way you make your choices," and "how you implement your actions." The vast majority of us have a little bit of us in each one of the categories. Some people are clearly more dominant in one or the other, while others can actually be somewhat neutral. Timing of the test and what is going on in someone's world can also impact results. The most important thing to remember is that there is no such thing as a good or a bad outcome. It is just a communication tool to better understand yourself and those around you. (Note, I am not a certified Myers-Briggs expert; this is my interpretation and how I use the tool.)

1.) The first letters in Myers-Briggs are **Introvert** and **Extrovert** (I or E). This often gets confused for determining if someone is a quiet wall flower, or very outgoing personality. While these are elements of what Myers-Briggs is testing, it is actually testing a deeper element of where your energy and motivation comes from. Are you more driven to follow the beat of your own drummer? That would make you an introvert. Are you someone who gets more energy from rallying the troops and being part of the team or group? Those people are considered extroverted. When I have taken the test, I am very close to the line between the two, because I like to follow the beat of my own drum, yet at the same time, I love for others to come along with me.

2.) The second letter in the Myers-Briggs analysis measures how we understand things. Some people are **Sensors** – (S). These people have a tendency to focus on all of the elements independently, whether they be sight, sound, smell, etc. They focus on being in the moment, but they extract each individual element. The other side of that coin are people that are **Intuitive** – (N). People that are intuitive assemble all the individual elements to create a big picture, and they use that picture to forecast the future. People who have "S" type personalities look at probabilities, while those who learn towards the "N" type speculate on possibilities.

3.) The third letter discusses the way you form judgments and make choices. Remember there is a little bit of both in all of us. However, the letter usually pertains to the way you are most natural or comfortable in making these choices. The **Thinker** (T) contains more of an analytical mindset and is somewhat detached in an objective fashion. It indicates that you make decisions and form conclusions in a logical and systematic manner. The **Feeler** (F) is more likely to make these choices based on likes and dislikes, and is somewhat more subjective in the way that conclusions are derived.

4.) The final letter focuses on your "action orientation" towards the outside world. Here you are either **Judging**

**(J)** or **Perceiving (P)**. Judging indicates that you approach the world with a plan. You tend to organize things and are focused on reaching some form of completion. The **Perceiver** (P) takes the world as it is and is more likely to be open minded and adapt to changing plans in a more expeditious fashion.

The grid below will give you some keywords to understand traits associated with each one of the Myers-Briggs categories:

### *Energy*

| Introvert (I) | Extravert (E) |
|---|---|
| Think, reflect, and then act | Act and then think/reflect |
| Requires "me time" to self-reflect to recharge themselves | Feels lonely when not attached to the outside world |
| Prefers one-on-one relationships | Enjoys a wide variety of people in their world |

### *Understanding*

| Sensing (S) | Intuitive (N) |
|---|---|
| Attends to the present and lives in the here and now | Often focused on the future and the possibilities ahead |
| Uses common sense to create practical solutions | Highly imaginative and creative, explores possibilities |
| Most comfortable when things are clear and precise | Comfortable with ambiguity, allowing for a creative process |

## Decision Making

| Feeling (F) | Thinking (T) |
|---|---|
| Focuses on the impact on people, relies on feelings and emotions | Looks for facts and logic |
| Consensus building | Relies upon dispassionate and critical analysis |
| Uneasy with conflict, negatively reacts to conflict | Conflict and disharmony are a normal part of interactions with others |

## Orientation Towards Action

| Perceiving (P) | Judging (J) |
|---|---|
| Takes action in real time | Plans in advance and executes against the plan |
| Loves multitasking | Very task oriented, and prefers to finish one thing before moving on to the next |
| Uses deadlines as a goal line, works best under pressure | Most comfortable using routines from the past that have been successful to manage ongoing projects and tasks |

If you have not done so already, please go online and do a quick Myers-Briggs assessment of yourself. It's the first step in understanding how to communicate to others. As I've told you, no matter what, there are 15 other possible combinations, so knowing yourself will help you understand others, because you now better understand your natural state. It will also help you communicate to others because you will see their natural state. The real benefit to Myers-Briggs is understanding the 15 other combinations so that you can see people's tendencies and communicate more effectively, after considering their tendencies.

There was a book written a few years ago titled, *"The Five Love Languages,"* written by Gary Chapman. In the book, Chapman details different ways people connect, and how, for example, if you're speaking one love language and someone else is speaking a different one, there can be a total disconnect, even though you both care about each other.

He describes these five languages shown below and what someone in that category needs to feel love.

- Words of Affirmation
  - encouragement, positive affirmations, and active listening
- Physical Touch
  - gentle touching and body language
- Receiving Gifts
  - thoughtful gifts (this does not mean you need to buy someone a new car every week), just the little things to show someone you're thinking of them
- Quality Time
  - uninterrupted time, creating special time, and one-on-one time
- Acts of Service
  - looks for phrases such as "let me help you," proving yourself as a true partner in their life

So, you're probably wondering, "Why am I telling you about love languages if this is a business book." The simple truth is building a business is about building relationships and nothing is more powerful than a loving relationship.

If you understand the person on the other side of the table and can speak their language, you will build successful and meaningful relationships. Going back to the concept of "people do business with us because they know us, like us, and trust us," what better way to build a relationship than to speak someone else's language?

Myers-Briggs and love languages, when used together, can give you a powerful advantage. I don't mean that you are taking advantage of someone; it's that you understand them and can communicate in a much tighter, more effective fashion. Your job as a leader is to keep people working towards a common goal and this is totally in line with that objective.

Think about creative ways that you can build relationships through better understanding yourself and understanding those around you. As an example, using Myers-Briggs, you are a sensor and you are talking to someone that is intuitive. Making a common-sense argument to someone who's highly imaginative might not be the best way to get their attention. Knowing that's how they receive information, you should look to paint a more creative picture in the future and bring them onto your side by helping them see it for themselves in an imaginative fashion.

Use the charts that I have provided. They will guide you in better ways to understand other people. In their language, others will use certain cues. If you are actively listening, you can observe these cues and capitalize on them. Someone who is a thinker will at some point in time ask for facts or analysis. You will literally hear those words. When that happens, you will be prepared.

## *Chapter 9: Picking a Partner*

If you are starting a company, picking the right partner(s) is one of the first steps. Pick right; your work life is great. Pick wrong; it will haunt you forever or end poorly. From the economics of the partnership to the dynamics of the relationship, the breath of the impact is almost immeasurable.

There is no perfect partnership; however, there are great partnerships. One of the core tenents needs to be trust. Another is alignment; seeing the world in the same way. Lastly, is space; the ability for each partner to have the space to do what they do best, to create value in the company.

The two most difficult conversations that have to happen early are "equity split" and "picking the CEO." These issues need to be resolved on day one of the creation of the partnership. If they are not resolved, they will tear the business apart, often before it starts. When driving a car, you cannot have four hands on the steering wheel. There needs to be a leader; someone who can make a final decision on issues, strategy, and direction. More importantly, know when to rally the team around an action and get things started. There is no value in an idea, unless it is supported by action. As former President Harry Truman once said so eloquently when talking about his role as the leader of the free world at the time, "The buck stops here." At some point in time, there must be a person who says, "Okay, here is what we are going to do, now let's execute." At that point, there can be no dissention, there can be no mixed messages, and there can be no alternate plans. Everyone must be on the same page.

There are key elements that partners need to see in a similar fashion. What they are trying to build, meaning the products or services. What they are trying to build, meaning a life-style business, or a business to sell in a few years. What they are trying to build, meaning a big company or a small company. These common elements form the base of the vision and relationship. There are key elements that should not overlap, but instead be complementary. Think Yin and Yang. They go together, but look different, and occupy their own space.

If partners all add the same value, then their roles overlap. Thus, their work is not additive to the value of the company. Partners should focus on $1 + 1 = 3$. What I am saying is that while each person is awesome, together they should create more value than just their individual contributions. To accomplish this, each partner has a genius that must be leveraged. Each partner needs to have roles and responsibilities that capitalize on their individual strengths and skills.

This is not to say that both partners can't have the same skills. Partners need to appreciate what the other partner is great at, while being supportive of each other. They need to have a common language, meaning they need to understand each other. This also means they have a trust that allows each to succeed, without trying to occupy the same space. From an economics perspective, if both partners are doing the same thing, the cost doubles.

With the exceptions of the "equity splits" and "picking the CEO," most of these principles apply to picking team members, as well.

Communicating your expectations and making sure people know the direction they need to go, are universal truths. Supporting them to be successful is a big part of their job satisfaction and your success. If you pick the right people, which is not easy, let them flourish. Give them the space, encouragement, and resources to grow!

There must be a common language. As stated numerous times, communication is key. Words matter, so you must make sure that the words you use have the same definitions. While that sounds easy, sometimes it is not. For an example, we throw the word "Margin" around a lot when we are measuring a company's performance. Is everyone on the same page with all the costs/expenses that go into the margin calculation. If its not clear, you will end up talking at someone, not with them because you don't have the same baseline understanding of the topic.

Nothing can be as destructive as having different work ethics between partners and team members. If one person is clearly putting in more effort and work, it can be a real point of contention. I strongly suggest that these issues are addressed early and revisited often. If partners resent each other, if left unaddressed, this will be felt throughout the organization and everyone will be put in uncomfortable situations, conversations and ultimately become unproductive or chose to leave.

## Chapter 10: Get over it, you are in Sales!

You are in sales. Everything a leader does includes an element of selling. Sales is not a dirty word! You are selling your team members ideas, you are selling customers products and services, you are selling lenders on why they should let you borrow money, and you are selling investors on why the equity in your organization is going to increase in value.

Now that I've told you everything is sales, I am asking you to stop selling. Your real goal is to create buyers. You want people to buy your products, buy into your ideas, and buy the fact that you know what you're doing. There is a subtle difference between everything is sales and creating buyers. The truth is, buyers are on a mission with a purpose. When you're in selling mode, you often end up discounting, because when you're selling, you're in closing mode. When you create a buyer, their desire for whatever it is that you're selling becomes equal or greater than your desire to sell; they will actually pay a premium and be more engaged.

A prime example of this can be seen every day in the stock market. When a lot of people are selling a stock, the price actually goes down. When there's good news and people flood into buying the stock, the price goes up. There is a greater desire by the buyers to buy in, while the sellers get the opportunity to capitalize on the buyers' desire. That's exactly what I'm advising you to do - create buyers!

A crucial element in creating buyers is becoming a great storyteller. Facts and numbers are critical elements of any story. We are all wired to listen and get emotionally involved in a good story. It's actually in our genetic makeup. Jeff Bezos, the founder of Amazon, uses storytelling as a very important tool. Prior to management meetings, he wants a narrative or a story written and circulated to attendees. This goes against the common practice of circulating a PowerPoint presentation or a list of bullet points. He is capitalizing on the power of the emotional connection to a story.

Creating buyers also means putting the person on the other side of the table first. While this sounds complicated, it actually means you need to focus on making the people that you are dealing with feel important and that you always have their best interest at heart. You cannot fake this. It needs to become a part of who you are. In addition, the skills of active listening and building trust are the elements that lead to desirable outcomes.

You've probably heard the expression, you don't get a second chance at making a first impression. This is true on many levels. You do, however, have the power of the honest apology to counteract this problem. It needs to be genuine and, more importantly, you need to understand what went wrong in order to fix it and make the apology sincere. It is critical when you are selling and creating buyers that you put your best foot forward and you make it easy for them to buy your ideas or your products.

A little trick here is to start a relationship off with a good question and then listen to the answer. These questions may be as simple as "What I can do for you?" or "What outcome you are looking for?" Sometimes, a simple statement will work, such as, "Tell me how you define success." These conversation starters show caring for the person on the other side of the table and gives you valuable information about their perspective as you build the relationship.

Once you get the conversation going, don't have a knee-jerk reaction to whatever is said. Take a moment and think before you speak. That first answer will be the one on which you are judged. After that, you are either building off of a strong platform or you are backpedaling. Clearly, there's only one direction you want to go. Here again, your experience is crucial. Think about how others have treated you in that situation. They say that imitation is the sincerest form of flattery. That's only true when someone did a good job, so that you are imitating success.

Remember, always word your replies in a positive fashion. Below is a small list that might help you better understand what I am saying.

- "I don't know" is a very limited response and can get other people to lose faith in you as opposed to saying, "That's a great question, let me do some research and I will get back to you immediately." By acknowledging the question in a positive fashion and letting people know that you are thoughtful about getting them the right answer, as well as a timely one, you will make them feel more connected.

- "Nope, I can't do it that way." Do you really think that's a sentence that anyone wants to hear? How about replace that with "In our experience, there might be a better way to handle this. May I tell you about it?"

- "I'm busy" is very off-putting. A better way to say this might be "I am just finishing something, if you give me a few moments, you will have my undivided attention."

Other ways to work from the positive include body language and small behavioral cues. As a kid, I worked at Baskin-Robbins serving ice cream. I learned an amazing lesson when I was there about exceeding customer expectations. Let's start off with the concept that a pint of ice cream is a pint of ice cream. It's a specific amount that's clearly measurable. When my boss taught me how to scoop ice cream, he always told me put about 90% of the ice cream into the pint so the pint looks full, and then put in one more scoop. This way the customer experiences that you're giving them a little extra. He went on to say, never overfill the pint and then cut the excess off. In both scenarios, you are giving the customer exactly what they ordered. However, by scooping off the top level, you're creating a level of disappointment that's not even factual, but rather emotional. By putting that last little bit in, you're making your customer, or your buyer, believe that you care about them and will go the extra mile.

This has been such a powerful lesson in my life. I always try to make someone feel special, even if I'm not giving more than what they expected. But, it's the appearance that counts. We've all heard the expression, perception is reality. While that concept is frustrating, it is exceptionally true.

Lastly, never talk through the sale! Another way of saying this is, often, less is more. When the person on the other side of the table shows signs of interest and acceptance, it's time for you to shut the F up! From that point forward, all you can do is move backwards, because they have already bought in. Additional information might actually work against you. This also means never be scared of silence. Often the sound of silence is scary, and people tend to jump into that void. Don't make that mistake. Use silence as a powerful tool; if your customer or team member has a question, they'll ask it. Don't fall into the trap of, "let me give you more answers" before that question has been asked.

The last and most important lesson in this chapter and in life is a combination of "showing up" and "being prepared."

Showing up is not about being in the room, it's about being present. It combines active listening with situational awareness. An example here might be from when I played basketball. As a guard, my job was to find the open person and help them score. Part of being present was knowing where everyone was on the court at any given time. Also, it was anticipating where they were going to be when I released the ball. Often, if I were to try to throw the ball where someone was, by the time it got there, they had already made a move and that's not where they were any longer. Being present is more than showing up, it means being aware of what's going on.

Nothing good happens just from showing up, unless you show up prepared. Always do your homework. Beware if you ask questions and you don't know what the answers might be, you will end up in an awful place. Always know who the person on the other side of the table is, learn what they like, learn how they think, and look at their history to know how they will behave. That way, you won't be surprised, and you can know where they're heading before they do, or at least when they get there. This will give you a competitive advantage, while also building trust. It will be clear that you've taken an interest in that person.

Great salespeople always keep the endgame in mind. They focus on finding the result they seek while simultaneously analyzing what it takes to satisfy their client or customer. There is great power in knowing what the goal is and keeping it in mind during the entire conversation. It can keep the conversation on track and reminds you when to stop, because you've already arrived.

In a corporate environment, understanding the expression "analysis paralysis" is fundamental. This is when an organization gets stuck searching for more data and looking at more options. If you know your goal and you get people to the goal line, be grateful for the score. Part of creating buyers is letting them know when they're ready. Too soon, and they walk away. While, if you wait too long, they will inevitably lose interest.

The last thing I will say about sales and creating buyers is that **time kills all deals**. Once again, I'm bringing the "C" word into the conversation - clock. A good salesperson knows when to ask for the order. A good leader knows when to end the discussion and begin the taking action phase.

Remember, a sale is not a sale until the customer pays the bill. A decision has no value until you actually execute against that decision. The key to success is always remembering that there is no value in ideas and discussions alone; you have to turn them into action. Always be action oriented and focus on getting things accomplished.

## Chapter 11: Pitching for Success

An integral part of selling is pitching. As a leader, you're always pitching something, whether it is your products or your ideas. This chapter deals with some of the tricks of the trade in the pitch world. I am talking more about pitching in front of a group of people, but the same tactics and techniques apply in one-on-one environments. The outcome of a Perfect Pitch is the building of a partnership of some kind. It's aligning your needs and those of others to build something greater. Great pitchers know how to put the pieces together to create a winning story.

Most people's number one fear is public speaking; it's even higher on the list then death. An example of this unique observational ability would be best said by Jerry Seinfeld (and I am paraphrasing): *If you are doing a eulogy at a funeral, and you fear public speaking, you're having a worse day than the poor guy in the box.*

For the purpose of this chapter, I will be using the words "pitch" and "present" or "pitch deck" and "presentation" interchangeably. Whether you are pitching to a fund-raising audience or presenting new concepts to your internal team, the skill sets, and requirements are identical.

Rule one for public speaking and pitching is, get over it, you're pitching. You're in the game, so now you have a binary outcome. You did it or you didn't do it. The best way to get over this fear is to practice, practice, practice. The more you know your stuff and are comfortable with the material, the easier it is to stand up in front of the room and let it fly.

When crafting the pitch, remember, you are designing a story. It has to have a beginning, middle, and an end. It has to be engaging and, at the same time, educational around whatever the topic of the pitch might be. Your goal is to keep your audience emotionally involved with the story so that you can take them on a journey and deliver them to whatever endpoint or goal that you have decided best defines success.

Before you even pitch, the first thing you need to do is know your definition of success. Clarity as to the definition of success is critical, because when designing a pitch, it's sometimes easier to start with the end in mind. Part of that design with the end in mind includes anticipating the questions that you will be asked, so that you can answer them along the way, which only makes you look that much smarter. Gaining respect from the people on the other side of the table is the fastest way to get to "yes" on anything that you pitch. Just remember, the questions come from the perspective of the audience, so think about what they might not understand or what their perspective might be, including their desires, and try to meet them.

Some of the main topics that you need to be prepared for include:

- What is the problem you're trying to solve?
- What's in it for the audience/participants?
- Why should the audience/participants care?
- Why are you (the presenter) attached to whatever your pitch is about?
- Do you, the presenter, have the right experience or team to be successful?

- Do you have examples showing when others have been successful or examples that are relevant and that prove you are on the right track?
- When pitching to get money, either budget or investment, the questions might include:
  - How are you going to make money based on the investment you seek?
  - How, and approximately when, will the potential investor get their money back?

I am often asked: "What is the best style for a presentation? Should I use slides? Should my pitch be scripted? Should I have handouts?" The answer is both simple and complex at the same time. You need to know your audience and what they expect. Meanwhile, you must also know yourself and your strengths. If you are not authentic, your audience will instantly know it. As a result, you will have lost credibility before the pitch has even started.

You should also design your pitch with time in mind. How long will your meeting be? How much time do you need to leave for questions and answers? When you can answer those two questions, then you can start really deciding your best approach.

I often start designing a pitch with a combination of both the story that I want to tell and deciding the difference between the important information that I need to deliver and the interesting information that might support what's truly important. This way, I make sure that I hit all of the important topics in the time allotted. Then, depending on my use of time in the actual meeting or pitch, I can throw in all of the interesting elements, if time permits.

This begs the question: "How do you know the difference between what is important and what is interesting?" Once again, if you have your endgame in mind, it will become clear where the line is between important and interesting.

If you are creating a presentation deck, it will become clear what points are important. When you make your bullet points, you usually want to use the first line for the important information. For interesting material, it is best to use the sub-bullets beneath the main point.

When creating a deck, keep in mind the people on the other side of the table. I know I use this expression a lot, but successful leaders and business people always have their audience, customers, and team members in mind when they speak.

We all absorb information in different ways. The two major ways can be segmented by what is referred to as right-brained and left-brained people. People who are right-brained have a tendency to be more creative and learn visually, because they're thinking about possibilities. People that are left-brained are often more likely to be impressed with facts and figures. This also goes back to our Myers-Briggs example.

When I create decks, I always make two boxes on every page. On one side of the page, I place words or bullet points. On the other side of the page, I put a relevant graphic or photo. This way, I am addressing both right-brained and left-brained people at the same time, keeping my entire audience engaged during the presentation or pitch. By now, I am sure you have noticed how I have used that technique in the design of this book.

Here's another tip: a good presentation shows an understanding of the relationship between the presenter and the deck. If you are a sports fan, you understand the relationship between the play-by-play announcer and the color commentator. This is similar to the relationship between a presenter and the presentation deck. The presenter does either the play-by-play, which I think is the better approach, or the color commentary. The deck plays the other role.

Presentation decks should be clean, with relatively few words. This is both for simplicity of conveying the message and for making the slides visually appealing.

When presenting, never, ever, ever read your slides to the audience. It's a good assumption that the people you present to, whether they be customers, team members, or investors, know how to read. If you read them your slides, you will be both boring them and disrespecting them. That means, in essence, you are 0 for 2 in achieving your goals, even before you really started.

Sometimes, you will use a team to do a presentation. If that's the case, check your ego at the door. Always have the best presenter do the presentation. If someone has a good rhythm, a style that is likable, and knows the subject, there's no reason not to have them do the presentation. It does not matter who presents, but it always matters that the presentation or pitch is well received. As a leader, you need to understand you have lots of tools at your disposal, this includes using your team in the best way possible. If one person is the best presenter, why not put them in a position to do a great job and help you achieve your goals?

If you have multiple presenters, you need to present with clarity, unity, and demonstrate chemistry. This means everyone is on the same page, in their thoughts and their goals about the pitch. Never, ever, disagree with a presenter on your team during the pitch. Remember, there is always doubt on the other side of the table, regardless of how much they might trust you individually. The moment that the people on the other side of the table see dissension in the presentation team, it becomes almost impossible to achieve your goal, whatever that goal may be. If someone misspeaks during a presentation, you can clean it up at the end, but don't throw a fellow presenter under the bus. You are one team on one mission. Support your team members, while at the same time, making sure the people to whom you are presenting get the most accurate information and the clearest picture possible.

No matter what you do in business, integrity, honesty, and alignment are critical. In particular, this is highlighted when pitching in front of an audience. You and/or your presentation team are in the spotlight. Treat the people on the other side of the table how you would want to be treated. In other words, make sure you are doing it right for the right reasons.

When you get to the question and answer period, even if you think the answer to a question was already answered during the presentation, you answer it anyway. Respect every question and say to people "thanks for the question" or "that's a great question," and then proceed to answer the question. You should be emotionally grateful on the inside that people have taken enough of an interest to dive deeper and inquire. If you can demonstrate gratitude during Q&A, it will be well received by your audience. If you're asked an unanticipated question, or one that you do not have the answer readily at hand, an honest response is critical. Be right up front and say something to the effect of "That's a great question, but I want to do a deeper dive into the information and I will get back to you with the answer." That kind of answer can build credibility, because, here too, the people on the other side of the table will appreciate that you are not trying to bluff them.

Lastly, have fun when you're doing a presentation or a pitch. Bring your "A" game to the party, and make sure it shows. If you are having fun and are highly energetic, the people to whom you are pitching will find that energy addictive and it will be more likely that they will become engaged during the pitch.

# Chapter 12: The Balanced Scorecard

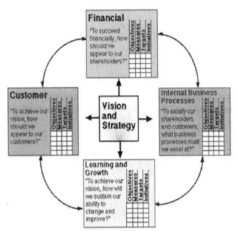

The balanced scorecard is a communication tool and strategy device to keep everyone in an organization aware of its goals, vision, as well as specific tasks and measurements to help achieve the mission. The term was originally developed at a medium-sized technology company in Boston named "Analog Devices." Later, it was codified in a book by Robert S. Kaplan and David P. Norton. They refer to the balanced scorecard as "translating strategy into action."

I used the balanced scorecard in companies where I was the CEO or with consulting clients. I found the tool helped the team think through all the elements and impacts of new initiatives. The balanced scorecard, for me, puts a process around the **development** and **implementation** of new initiatives.

Companies that use the balanced scorecard find that people from all over the organization get aligned and better understand their roles and responsibilities within the ecosystem of the entire company. It was designed with the understanding that everything connects and that the people inside the organization achieve goals by detailing their role in the bigger picture.

The balanced scorecard not only outlines a company's vision and mission, but also, gives specific goals, measurements, and assigns responsibility to an individual to oversee these elements. By combining vision, mission, and goals with accountability, it's easy to measure both progress and see areas inside an organization that need additional attention or a course correction.

The balanced scorecard can be designed as a graphic to communicate the high-level elements.

The balanced scorecard process starts with detailing a strategy and vision. Surrounding that vision and strategy, the balanced scorecard model looks at the organization from four different perspectives. Financial, internal business process, learning and growth, and customers. Any initiative or goal that a company sets for itself impacts all four of these areas.

Supporting each of these four perspectives are:

- **Objectives**
  - In the objective section for each perspective, the objective from that perspective is detailed out in great specificity.
- **Measurements**
  - Once the objectives are defined, a specific set of measurements to track progress also needs to be defined.
- **Targets**
  - The targets to find the outcomes of success. They are specific in nature, so that everyone knows the goal line that they are driving towards.
- **Initiatives**
  - The initiatives are a list of tactics that will be implemented in order to achieve the goals.
- **Ownership**
  - Ownership speaks to an individual, as well as to the team. Every element should have a "champion" or "owner." While a team owns an initiative together, ownership speaks to the person that is leading the

charge. If there is not one person that is accountable, that means everybody is responsible, and nobody is accountable.

Let's talk about a company with the vision of increasing revenue from each of their top ten customers. With that vision in mind, let's take a trip around the balanced scorecard. While this vision is being driven by the board room, sales leadership would be tasked to run this through the balanced scorecard process to make sure everything is in alignment before the rollout of the new initiative to the organization.

This is what makes the balanced scorecard so productive. In this case, the process is as important as the product. We will plan all the elements that need to occur to ensure successful execution against the vision. All of the elements will have been thought through and then can be rolled out and communicated to the organization.

In the example below, senior management has made the sales leader the accountable party to drive this initiative.

- **Financial**: The company has set the goal of 7% more revenue from each of the top ten customers.
  - The first question might be, how much revenue is that?
  - How much will the company budget for marketing materials and additional customer support to manage that new business?
  - How will this increase or change compensation packages?
  - Will the company need to invest in additional software to manage customer data to make good decisions that lead to this additional revenue?

- **Business Process**: Sales management will need to know more about the customers to drive a planning process. This will require the individual salespeople to share information about their customers that they are not currently sharing.
    - The company will have to have systems in place to handle all of the additional information needed to better understand their customers.
    - There will need to be an incentive system in place to get the sales team to give up their grip on owning the customers and, instead, allow the company to own the customers. This battle between salespeople and the company as to who owns the customer has been going on for years and years. Salespeople often believe that their power is in hoarding the information about customers. The truth is, the company needs to own the customer and the salespeople should not be allowed to hinder that process.
    - Should there be an internal resource to make sure the new database is being properly maintained by the sales team?
    - Should a process be established by which the CEO makes semi-regular calls to each of these top ten customers, just to say hello and ask how things are going? These types of calls build rapport and relationships between the company and its customers that goes deeper than just having a salesperson on the account.
- **Learning**: The company will need to decide which team members are part of this initiative and the best modality to train people as to what needs to happen.
    - Technology Training

- How do salespeople use new tools at their disposal?
- How does management learn how to retrieve information to better contact customers?
  - Corporate culture:
    - How do you present this change to the salespeople and get them to be cooperative in sharing the information?
    - How do you get the internal people, including customer service and management, to understand the value of this information, and how to use it in conjunction with the sales force to best identify additional opportunities?
- **Customers**: The impact on the customer must be subtle, or the customer might feel that the company has become too aggressive.
  - What will the customer experience be like? Will more people reach out to them?
  - Should the customer be told that the company is taking more ownership and that the team on their account is growing to provide better service?

The process I have just described is the beginning of the balanced scorecard. First, you go around the circle and think about all of the questions. After developing answers to these essential questions, targets are then designed, and goals are set. Then, you go around the circle and design specific initiatives and measurements as to the progress of the initiatives and name an accountable party who takes ownership of that initiative to see that it is properly implemented.

The balanced scorecard can be used to think through any initiatives to make sure all the constituencies have a voice in the planning and ownership through execution. It lowers the number of elements that might otherwise fall through the cracks.

Once the balanced scorecard is finished, it then becomes a great communication tool. The entire organization can then see the vision and the tactics that the company is using on any one initiative. They can also see that the entire company, including the departments they don't work for, are supporting the initiative. It creates a community and, at the same time, helps each individual employee recognize and believe that they are not alone or the only person working hard.

You can also use the balanced scorecard to better design your career choices. You can think through all of these elements, from financial goals to the process of identifying additional things you need to learn, and how the balanced scorecard impacts your customers, who may actually be your supervisors and managers.

The reason I like the balanced scorecard is that it puts a process and a mindset in place, which helps me think things through in a deeper and more organized fashion. Lastly, someone in the organization takes responsibility for every initiative; this ownership increases involvement, accountability and participation across all departments. It is possibly one of the best tools I have ever used to build a business.

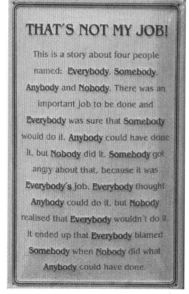

**THAT'S NOT MY JOB!**

This is a story about four people named: Everybody, Somebody, Anybody and Nobody. There was an important job to be done and Everybody was sure that Somebody would do it. Anybody could have done it, but Nobody did it. Somebody got angry about that, because it was Everybody's job. Everybody thought Anybody could do it, but Nobody realised that Everybody wouldn't do it. It ended up that Everybody blamed Somebody when Nobody did what Anybody could have done.

# Chapter 13: The Final Critical Stuff

## The SMART plan

Be SMART when setting goals! As we have discussed, it is critical to have a plan, vision, and direction. Part of that includes setting your goals. I recommend the smart approach.

The more specific you can make your goals, the easier it will be for you to stay on track. This ties into the concept of "if you can't measure it, you can't manage it." By being specific with your goals, you can create measurements to see how your progress is going. It's often said: "Go big or go home." However, when you're setting goals, keep them in the realm of attainability. Setting goals that are truly not achievable is not helpful or effective. You can always set a new goal after you achieve the first goal. This ties into the old saying of "How do you eat an elephant? One bite at a time." If you set attainable goals, you will feel like a success when you achieve them. Success begets more success. Setting yourself up for failure is never a good thing. Making your goals relevant to your ultimate objective not only helps you measure your progress, but also, keeps you on track and heading in the correct direction. Finally, set deadlines. Everyone has a tendency at times to procrastinate. By having a specific deadline, it helps keep you focused on the end game.

**No Blue Bagging Corporate Culture**

Another one of our Cs is **Culture**. Creating a healthy corporate culture combines the proper treatment of customers, both internal and external, and a great code of conduct that manages interactions. For example, a code of conduct when you have a dog, is to clean up the dog's mess, often referred to as "blue bagging." Your organization is made up of people, not dogs, which is why the organization should not be tolerant of "blue bagging." If someone in the organization makes a mess, it's critical that person takes responsibility for cleaning up his or her mess. That's not to say that person cannot solicit help and input from others, but, they need to take the lead and deal with the consequences. If your corporate culture is one that allows people to blame and walk away from problems they create, your company will become incredibly toxic and it will lead to an environment in which this kind of behavior will become rampant. Give praise, not for the mistakes that someone makes, but for the fact that they stayed on top of it and remediated whatever problems occurred.

**Proofread Your Work**

I believe this one stands on its own. People will question your skills and intelligence when you send emails, presentations, or other documents with spelling errors. It's even worse when you send a document and the little red squiggly lines are still underneath the words, showing that you knew better, and let it slide anyway. As I said before, do the right thing for the right reasons! Always put your best foot forward!

**You Control Your Own Attitude and Effort**

In life and in business, there are some things that are in our control,

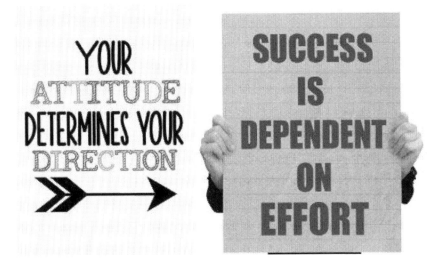

and other things that are not. Regardless of that, two things that are always in your control are your attitude and your effort. No one can change those things; they are yours, and yours alone. Nothing good ever comes from having a bad attitude, while great things often come when you put the appropriate effort into something. Using these things in tandem will show your team that you're a natural leader and give them one more reason to follow you.

## Output and Outcomes

These two words are closely connected; however, they are dramatically different. Understanding this difference makes planning and measuring much better. Output is how you measure the things that you do, outcome is the result.

A great example of this can be seen when you're measuring "market share." Market share is often seen as a very important measuring tool.

It helps one understand the position a company occupies in the marketplace. It can give some insights into where the company can grow and how big it can get. Market share is a measurement of an **outcome**. If the company communicates properly to the marketplace, it develops the right products or services and, thus, delivers a great customer experience that will likely drive market share growth. These behaviors are the **output** of what the organization is doing. By driving the right set of outputs, dramatic increases in success will follow. After all, driving success is the ultimate outcome.

## Don't Play People!

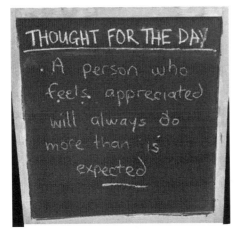

THOUGHT FOR THE DAY
. A person who feels appreciated will always do more than is expected

Both as a leader and a manager, it's critically important to get the most out of your team. This means you need to make sure they understand their roles, and that you create an environment in which they want to follow you. You need to keep them motivated, even when times get tough. It's easy to forget that people are people when you get so focused on the task at hand. It's important that you appreciate the people who help you achieve your mission. This is not playing them, it's respecting them!

## Know Your Numbers

Always be prepared. Do your homework on who you are meeting and know why you are part of the meeting. Now that you know that important stuff, **know your numbers.**

Here is where it gets complicated. What numbers? You always need to know the basics. When you go into a meeting, you need to understand what's important to your audience. If you are speaking to an investor, it's the numbers surrounding a return on investment (ROI). If you are speaking with a team member, you need to know the numbers that impact them. Focus on the numbers that explain where you are, and where you want to be. These are the numbers you will hold them accountable for delivering.

## Occam's Razer

Occam's razor is a principal often used in science for problem solving. Its basic tenant is that the simplest explanation tends to be the right one. Another way of looking at it would be when making a hypothetical argument or examining a potential initiative, look for a course that has the fewest assumptions in order to get to the right answer. The example

most often used is: when you hear hoof beats, think horses, not zebras. In the business world, when you confront a problem, there is often a simple explanation that leads to the root cause. Focus there first, in order to maximize your resources.

## Patience and Wisdom

Often, we work under stressful deadlines. If we allow the pressures of time to cloud our judgment, it's more likely that we will make mistakes. This comes into play in two ways. When setting a deadline, take a moment to think if it is arbitrary or specific. It's critical to know the difference between the two.

When a customer tells you, they need something by the 3$^{rd}$ of next month, that is a very specific deadline. Before you accept the order, it's worth taking a moment to see if that is even possible to achieve. If it is, muster the resources to get it done. If it's not, communicate to the customer the issues and find another way to make that date work. It may be a price concession by the customer in order for you to pay for overtime, or it might be a partial delivery because they don't need everything. Be creative.

Sometimes, we set a date because we don't want things to go too long. As a result, a due date is arbitrary. Ask yourself, why did I pick that date and is that what's best for the company? Everything takes time and remind yourself of the "C" word - clock. Time is a perishable asset. For that reason, it needs to be used wisely.

Almost always, being patient and waiting for the right moment to best utilize your time and resources is the best decision. You can never go wrong by being thoughtful and prioritizing what's important over what's interesting.

## *Chapter 14: Success is Not a Trick, It's a Process*

Recall the old saying from earlier: "How do you eat an elephant? One bite at a time." That's an excellent analogy to: How do you build a career and how you build a business?

Success is not a trick. Magic happens because the magician has practiced, knows the art, and uses the tools to his or her advantage.

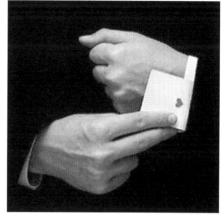

In this book, I detailed a combination of tools and stories that help explain the mindset that will prepare you for success.

Building a career and building a business is like being a juggler; you have to have a lot of balls up in the air and know exactly where they are. My goal is to help you better understand that ecosystem.

It rarely takes one bad thing to destroy a business and it rarely takes just one good thing to build it. When it comes to a career, with the exception of losing your integrity, everything can be worked through. It's all about the strategy you choose to deploy.

Everything is connected. Everything needs to be managed, or it will run to disorder. Make sure you understand the critical success factors at play when you're chasing success. Look for the key performance indicators so that you know you're on track. Focus on what's truly important and start with the impact of the 7Cs. Put yourself in the mindset of understanding not just the people on the other side of the table, but also, understanding yourself. All of these elements work well together, and I promise, if you use them over and over, your muscle memory will kick in and you will see dramatic changes in your career and your business.

*"I cannot teach anybody anything, I can only make them think."* **Socrates**

The goal of my book is to make you think and learn. While I have the title, "professor" is easy to profess, to put ideas out in the universe and hope people get something from most of them.

I believe being a teacher is a higher calling. However, I don't know if I'm a teacher until I know my students are thinking for themselves and have learned something along the way. I hope that something has occurred inside of you from reading my words, and that you truly take them to heart. If you do incorporate my lessons into your personal and professional life, then I have been successful in my mission, and you will be successful in yours.

### ***Thank you!***

*Appendix: Really Awesome Videos on YouTube*

- **Jamaican Animals Walk United (1:29)**
https://www.youtube.com/watch?v=q3Mb56JX7Yk
This short video shows the power of leadership in numerous ways. I love the second clip. Watch the lead ant direct the team and join in to help them. This animation demonstrates **leadership at its finest!**

- **Science of Persuasion (11:51)**
https://www.youtube.com/watch?v=cFdCzN7RYbw&t=8s
This video shows **"how to get to yes"** with customers through simple techniques to build credibility and persuade others towards your desired outcome.

- **Honda "Paper" (1:58)**
https://www.youtube.com/watch?v=fLCEd8xk1BE
This video is a look at decades of Honda's innovation, all of which starts with an engine. It is a clean and clear way to better understand the concept of **"Core Competence."**

- **What is the Role of CEO? By Dan Hoffman, Former CEO at M5 Networks, Inc (2:08)**
https://www.youtube.com/watch?v=24Io1uoi6i8&t=22s
In very concise terms, Dan Hoffman tells a story that shows the difference between what is **interesting** and what is **important**. He shows where leaders need to focus.

- **Inside the Mind of a Master Procrastinator | Tim Urban (14:04)**
https://www.youtube.com/watch?v=arj7oStGLkU&t=160s
The title says it best. Since one of my favorite "C"s is clock, you can learn a lot from Tim Urban.

- **Start with Why -- How Great Leaders Inspire Action |
  Simon Sinek | TEDxPugetSound  (18:01)**
  https://www.youtube.com/watch?v=u4ZoJKF_VuA
  This video is at the core of what I teach. It's been viewed
  around 5 million times and I think that's way too low. Start
  with why and you will live with passion. **Your followers will
  follow, and your customers will buy.**


  *Don't forget to visit "TheOneDayMBA.org"*

Made in the USA
San Bernardino, CA
15 April 2019